Deep Learning for Managers

TRANSFORMING LEADERSHIP IN THE AI ERA

Partha Majumdar

A

Copyright © 2024 Partha Majumdar

All rights reserved.

No part of this book may be reproduced, stored in a retrieval system, or transmitted in any form or by any means, electronic, mechanical, photocopying, recording, or otherwise, without express written permission of the author.

ISBN-13: 9798321991282

Cover design by Partha Majumdar.

Unless explicitly stated, all images are created by the author or licensed from Adobe.

Dedicated to my wife,

Deepshree Majumdar.

She does all the work at home and fixes infrastructure issues to earn money to run our house.

Preface

In an age where artificial intelligence is not just a buzzword but a fundamental driver of innovation, "Deep Learning for Managers: Transforming Leadership in the AI Era" serves as a beacon for managers navigating the complex waters of deep learning technology. This book demystifies the intricate world of artificial neural networks, algorithms, and their practical applications in business, all while minimizing the reliance on complex mathematical formulations.

Our journey through this book is designed to equip leaders, strategists, and decision-makers with the knowledge and insights necessary to harness the transformative power of deep learning. Whether at the helm of a tech startup or steering a division in a Fortune 500 company, the deep learning revolution has implications for your strategy, operations, and competitive edge.

"Deep Learning for Managers" is more than a guide; it's a companion in your leadership journey in the digital age. It synthesizes technical concepts, industry applications, ethical considerations, and strategic planning into a coherent narrative that resonates with the technically inclined and the uninitiated.

As we delve into the chapters, I aim to illuminate the path for integrating deep learning into your organizational fabric, from assembling a capable team to navigating the ethical landscape of AI. This book is your guide to surviving and thriving in the era of deep learning, transforming challenges into opportunities for innovation and growth.

Welcome to the future of management, where deep learning and leadership converge to redefine what's possible in business and beyond.

Partha Majumdar

d

Table of Contents

PREFACE .... B

1. THE MOTIVATION BEHIND DEEP LEARNING 1

    HUMAN ENDEAVOR AND ARTIFICIAL INTELLIGENCE 1
    UNDERSTANDING THE NATURAL NERVOUS SYSTEM 3
    FROM BIOLOGICAL TO ARTIFICIAL NEURAL NETWORKS 6
    CONCLUSION 10

2. FOUNDATIONS OF NEURAL NETWORKS 11

    STRUCTURE OF AN ARTIFICIAL NEURAL NETWORK (ANN) 12
    ARCHITECTING NEURAL NETWORKS 15
    TRAINING NEURAL NETWORKS: THE HEART OF LEARNING 19
    PRACTICAL IMPLICATIONS FOR MANAGERS 21
    CONCLUSION 22

3. THE DEEP LEARNING REVOLUTION 25

    FROM ROOTS TO REVOLUTION 25
    THE DEMOCRATIZATION OF DEEP LEARNING 29
    IMPACT ACROSS INDUSTRIES 34
    CONCLUSION 38

4. UNDERSTANDING DEEP LEARNING ALGORITHMS 41

    CONVOLUTIONAL NEURAL NETWORKS (CNNS): THE VISIONARIES OF AI
    41
    RECURRENT NEURAL NETWORKS (RNNS): MASTERS OF SEQUENCE
    AND TIME 49
    AUTOENCODERS: THE ART OF DATA COMPRESSION AND
    RECONSTRUCTION 55

Generative Adversarial Networks (GANs): The Creators of the AI World 63
Conclusion 70

5. **DEEP LEARNING IN PRACTICE** **73**

Initiating a Deep Learning Project 73
Data Collection and Preparation 76
Choosing the Right Algorithm 80
Model Training and Fine-Tuning 84
Evaluating Model Performance 89
Addressing Common Challenges 93
Fostering a Collaborative and Continuous Learning Environment 96
Conclusion 100

6. **APPLICATIONS OF DEEP LEARNING IN BUSINESS** **103**

Finance: Revolutionizing Risk Management and Fraud Detection 103
Healthcare: Enhancing Diagnostics and Personalizing Treatment 108
Retail: Transforming Customer Experiences and Supply Chain Efficiency 113
Manufacturing: Predictive Maintenance and Quality Control 119
Challenges and Considerations 124
Conclusion 125

7. **NAVIGATING THE ETHICAL AND SOCIAL IMPLICATIONS 127**

Data Privacy: A Paramount Concern 127
Algorithmic Bias: Ensuring Fairness 132

THE IMPACT ON EMPLOYMENT: NAVIGATING THE TRANSITION 138
ETHICAL FRAMEWORKS AND GUIDELINES 143
CONCLUSION 145

8. MANAGING RISKS IN DEEP LEARNING PROJECTS 147

UNDERSTANDING THE RISKS 147
RISK ASSESSMENT AND MITIGATION STRATEGIES 148
FOSTERING A RISK-AWARE CULTURE 151
CONCLUSION 152

9. BUILDING A DEEP LEARNING TEAM 153

UNDERSTANDING THE DEEP LEARNING TEAM DYNAMICS 153
FOSTERING COLLABORATION AND CONTINUOUS LEARNING 155
CASE STUDY 1: TECH GIANT'S AI LAB 156
CASE STUDY 2: HEALTHCARE START-UP 161
CASE STUDY 3: FINANCIAL SERVICES FIRM 166
CONCLUSION 172

10. THE FUTURE OF DEEP LEARNING 173

ADVANCEMENTS IN NEURAL NETWORK ARCHITECTURES 173
TRANSFER LEARNING AND DEMOCRATIZATION OF AI 174
INTEGRATION WITH QUANTUM COMPUTING 174
PERSONALIZED AND PREDICTIVE MEDICINE 175
AUTONOMOUS SYSTEMS AND ROBOTICS 175
ETHICAL AI AND GOVERNANCE 176
THE IMPACT ON EMPLOYMENT AND EDUCATION 176
CONCLUSION 177

11. PREPARING YOUR ORGANIZATION FOR DEEP LEARNING 179

STRATEGIC PLANNING FOR DEEP LEARNING INTEGRATION 179

    BUILDING THE INFRASTRUCTURE FOR DEEP LEARNING 180
    CULTIVATING A CULTURE OF INNOVATION 181
    EXAMPLES OF ORGANIZATIONAL PREPARATION FOR DEEP LEARNING 182
    CONCLUSION 184

12. EMBRACING THE DEEP LEARNING ERA 187

    KEY TAKEAWAYS 187
    EMBRACING DEEP LEARNING IN YOUR ORGANIZATION 189
    CONCLUSION 191

ABOUT THE AUTHOR I

    BOOKS BY THE AUTHOR II

j

k

1. The Motivation behind Deep Learning

The journey into deep learning begins with a foundational understanding of how the human brain operates and how its principles have inspired the creation of neural networks, a core component of deep learning. This exploration satisfies our curiosity and equips managers with the knowledge to effectively harness deep learning in business applications.

Human Endeavor and Artificial Intelligence

The quest to imbue machines with human-like intelligence has been a long-standing ambition, culminating in the development of Artificial Intelligence (AI). AI aims to enable machines to perform tasks that typically require human intellect, such as reasoning, learning, and problem-solving. Unlike humans, computers were initially tasked with repetitive instructions, excelling in consistency and endurance. For instance, telecom companies have leveraged computers for tracking customer usage, known as Call Detail Records (CDRs) or XDRs, highlighting the computer's ability to follow predefined instructions without genuine 'thought.'

The progression toward intelligent networks (IN) marked a significant leap. IN enabled systems to make decisions based on predefined entitlements, enhancing the efficiency of services in telecommunications. However, these systems could not still 'think' independently while advanced.

The concept of machine learning introduced a paradigm where computers could learn from data, making informed decisions without explicit programming. This marked the beginning of computers 'thinking' by analyzing past data to optimize operations, such as determining the most efficient route for telecommunication networks, known as the Least Cost Routing problem.

Deep learning represents a further advancement in machine learning, employing neural networks that mimic the structure and function of the human brain. These networks consist of layers of artificial neurons that process and transmit signals, enabling machines to perform complex tasks with minimal human intervention. Deep learning encompasses the ability of machines to learn from vast amounts of data, draw insights, and make increasingly sophisticated decisions.

Understanding the Natural Nervous System

The inspiration for neural networks comes from nature, particularly the human brain, which is composed of billions of neurons. These neurons use electrical and chemical signals to communicate, with each neuron consisting of a nucleus (soma), dendrites (for receiving signals), and an axon (for transmitting signals). The interaction of ions across the neuron's membrane generates neural signals, with specific ion channels allowing the flow of ions like Sodium (Na+), Potassium (K+), Calcium (Ca++), and Chloride (Cl-), creating action potentials that propagate signals across the nervous system.

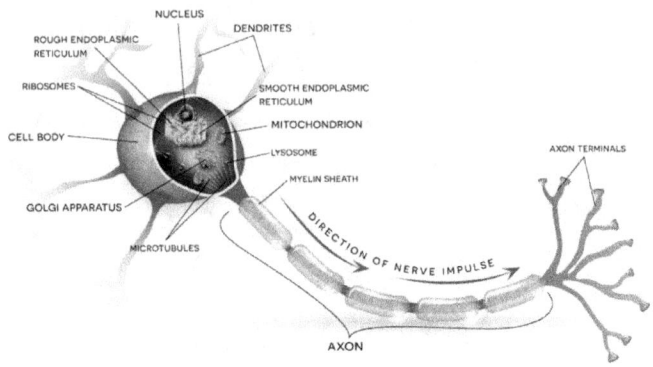

A Neuron in the Human Brain.

Neurons communicate at synapses, where one neuron's axon meets another's dendrites. Signals can be transmitted electrically for fast, bidirectional communication or chemically for unidirectional communication through neurotransmitters. Chemical synapses involve complex processes where neurotransmitters are released from the presynaptic cell to the postsynaptic cell, facilitating the transmission of signals across the synaptic cleft.

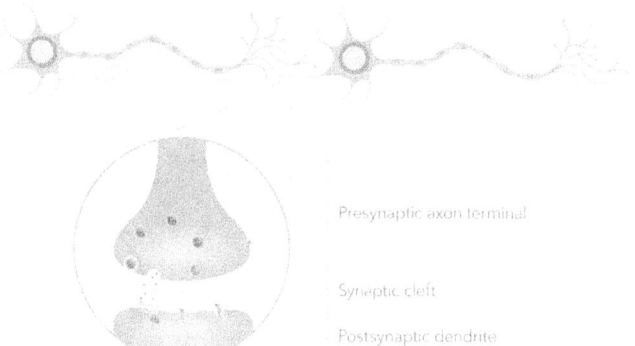

The Synapse is where two neurons meet and exchange signals.

The brain's network is intricate, with each neuron connecting to many others, forming a complex web that allows for the processing and transmission of signals. Neurons can perform convergence (integrating multiple signals), divergence (spreading signals to multiple neurons), and recurrence (feedback loops), contributing to the brain's ability to learn, remember, and adapt.

A fundamental principle in neuroscience, known as Hebbian learning, posits that neurons that fire together wire together, forming the basis of learning and memory. This principle underscores the adaptive nature of neural networks, both natural and artificial, highlighting the brain's ability to reorganize and strengthen connections based on experience.

From Biological to Artificial Neural Networks

The journey from the intricate workings of biological neural networks within the human brain to the conceptualization and development of artificial neural networks (ANNs) marks a significant milestone in the evolution of artificial intelligence. This transition represents a melding of biological inspiration and technological innovation, aiming to replicate the remarkable capabilities of the human brain in processing, analyzing, and interpreting information through artificial means. The foundational work by Warren S. McCullough and Walter Pitts in 1943 set the stage for a pivotal area of study and development in AI, culminating in the advanced deep learning algorithms we see today.

The endeavor to mimic the brain's capabilities led to McCullough and Pitts's conceptualization of artificial neural networks. Their model proposed a simplified version of a McCullough-Pitt neuron, which could perform binary operations. The model was based on the premise that each artificial neuron could receive multiple binary inputs (0s and 1s, akin to the inhibitory and excitatory impulses in biological neurons) and produce a single binary output based on a threshold activation function. This output would then serve as an input to subsequent neurons in the network, creating a cascade of binary operations that could simulate basic decision-making processes.

The McCullough-Pitt neuron comprised two main components: an aggregation function, which summed the weighted inputs, and an activation function, which determined the output based on whether the aggregated input exceeded a certain threshold. This structure was symbolic of the decision-making process within a biological neuron, where the integration of signals in the soma generates an action potential if a certain threshold is met.

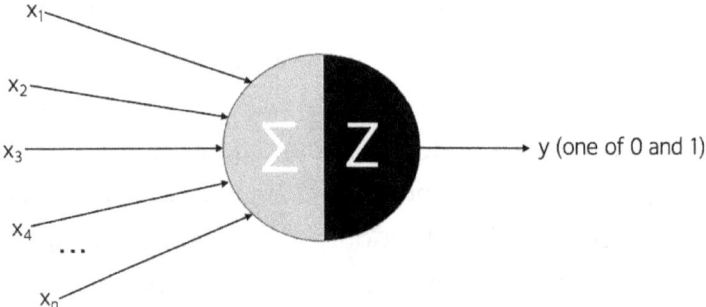

This is a conceptual model of a McCullough-Pitt Neuron. The neuron could take any number of binary inputs and produce a binary output. Σ denotes the summation function used to generate a weighted sum of the inputs. Z represents the activation function. Z acts on the output of Σ and is used to decide whether the signal will propagate.

The development of the McCullough-Pitt neuron model was a seminal moment in the history of AI, representing one of the first attempts to translate the principles of biological neural networks into a computational framework. This model laid the groundwork for subsequent advancements in neural network research, developing more complex and capable ANNs. Over the decades, ANNs have evolved from simple binary decision-makers to sophisticated networks capable of learning from vast amounts of data, recognizing patterns, and making predictions with remarkable accuracy.

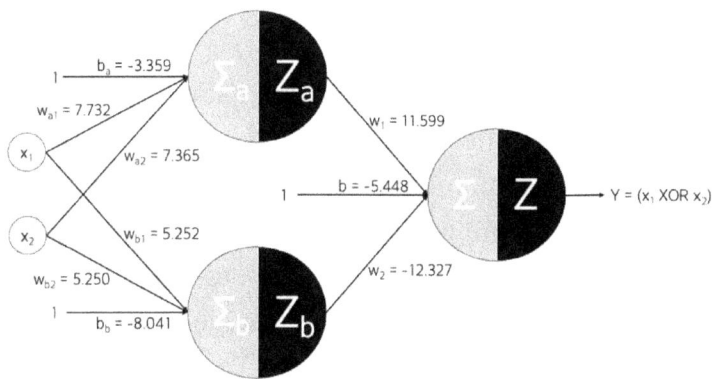

A simple Artificial Neural Network (ANN) performing XOR (eXclusive OR) operation.

Deep learning, a subset of machine learning, has emerged at the forefront of this evolution. ANNs are becoming deeper (comprising many layers) and more intricate, mirroring the depth and complexity of the human brain to some extent. Deep learning algorithms, powered by these advanced neural networks, can now perform tasks once thought to be the exclusive domain of human cognition, such as image and speech recognition, natural language processing, and even creative endeavors like art and music composition.

Conclusion

The implications of deep learning extend far beyond the technical underpinnings. Deep learning offers transformative potential for businesses, enabling sophisticated data analysis, predictive modeling, and autonomous decision-making systems. Managers must grasp these concepts to leverage deep learning effectively, driving innovation, efficiency, and competitive advantage in their organizations.

2. Foundations of Neural Networks

In modern technology, artificial neural networks (ANNs) stand as a cornerstone of deep learning, simulating the intricacies of human intellect. This chapter unfolds the essence of ANNs, tailored for managers keen on harnessing the transformative power of deep learning within their organizations.

The advent of artificial neural networks (ANNs) marked a pivotal moment in the evolution of computational models inspired by the intricate workings of the human brain. At the core of this revolutionary approach are artificial neurons, meticulously designed to simulate the functions of biological neurons. These artificial neurons serve as the fundamental units of data processing within neural networks, each tasked with receiving, processing, and transmitting information.

Structure of an Artificial Neural Network (ANN)

In the structure of an ANN, every artificial neuron acts as a critical junction, transforming input data into outputs that carry significant meaning for subsequent layers or the network's outcome. This transformation is achieved through weighted inputs, a bias term, and an activation function, which collectively determine each neuron's output.

Weights: The Essence of Learning

In neural networks, weights play a central role, analogous to the synapses in a biological brain. These weights represent the strength or influence of the connections between individual neurons within the network. The value of each weight signifies the impact of one neuron's output on another neuron's activation level, mirroring the synaptic efficacy in biological neural networks.

Learning in an ANN is fundamentally about adjusting these weights. During training phases, the network undergoes a series of weight adjustments based on discrepancies between the predicted outputs and the actual outcomes. This iterative process of fine-tuning the weights is driven by algorithms designed to minimize prediction errors, enhancing the network's overall predictive accuracy and decision-making capabilities.

Biases: Steering the Decision Path

Biases in ANNs are akin to the inherent tendencies or predispositions that influence human decision-making processes. Within neural networks, a bias term is added to the inputs of each neuron's activation function. This term ensures that a neuron has the potential to activate and contribute to the network's output, even in cases where all incoming inputs might be zero.

Including a bias term effectively shifts the activation function along the horizontal axis. This shift is crucial for the learning process, as it allows the activation function to be more flexible and adaptable, enabling the network to better capture and model complex patterns within the data.

Activation Functions: The Spark of Neural Activity

Activation functions are the heart and soul of neural networks, imbuing them with the ability to decide whether individual neurons should be activated based on the aggregated input signals. These functions introduce non-linearity into the network, a critical feature that allows ANNs to learn and model complex, non-linear relationships within data.

Among the various activation functions employed in neural networks, two of the most prevalent are the sigmoid and the Rectified Linear Unit (ReLU). The sigmoid function compresses the output of each neuron to a range between 0 and 1, making it particularly useful for models where outputs are interpreted as probabilities. On the other hand, the ReLU function permits only positive values to be passed to the next layer, effectively mimicking the "all-or-nothing" firing mechanism observed in biological neurons. This property of ReLU helps mitigate issues related to vanishing gradients, making it a favored choice in many deep-learning architectures.

The Interplay of Components in Neural Networks

The orchestrated interplay of artificial neurons, weights, biases, and activation functions forms the backbone of neural network models. Each component plays a distinct yet interrelated role in the network's ability to learn from data, make predictions, and perform myriad tasks ranging from simple classification to complex pattern recognition.

Architecting Neural Networks

The design of neural networks is a fascinating endeavor that mirrors the complexity and functionality of the human brain, albeit in a simplified and abstract form. At the heart of this endeavor lies the structuring of layers composed of artificial neurons, each with a unique role in the data processing pipeline.

Layers of Complexity

In the simplest terms, a neural network is organized into three primary types of layers: input, hidden, and output layers.

The input layer serves as the gateway to the network, where raw data is introduced for processing. This layer doesn't perform computations but instead passes the data to subsequent layers for analysis.

The hidden layers are considered the network's "brain." They undertake most computational tasks. These layers are where the network discerns patterns, relationships, and features within the data that might not be immediately apparent. The number and configuration of these hidden layers primarily define the depth and complexity of a neural network. A network with more hidden layers (a "deeper" network) can potentially model more complex phenomena but at the cost of increased computational demands and, often, more data for practical training.

The output layer is the culmination of the network's processing efforts, where the final decisions or predictions are made based on the analysis conducted by the preceding layers. The configuration of the output layer is closely tied to the specific task the network is designed to perform, be it classification, regression, or any other machine-learning task.

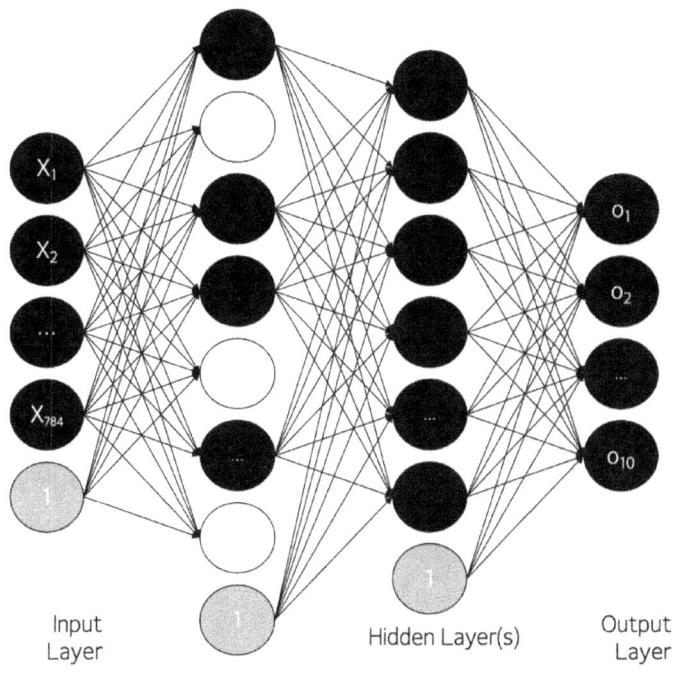

*This is an Artificial Neural Network (ANN) for classifying handwritten digits. The input is 28 * 28-pixel images, which translates to 28 * 28 = 784 inputs per image. This ANN has two hidden layers. Ten neurons are in the output layer for the ten possible decisions (digits 0 to 9).*

Design Considerations

Designing a neural network's architecture requires careful consideration of the task at hand and the nature of the input data. Factors such as the number of hidden layers, the number of neurons in each layer, and the connections between these neurons can significantly impact the network's performance. There is no one-size-fits-all architecture; each problem domain might necessitate a unique configuration tailored to the specific characteristics of the data and the desired outcome.

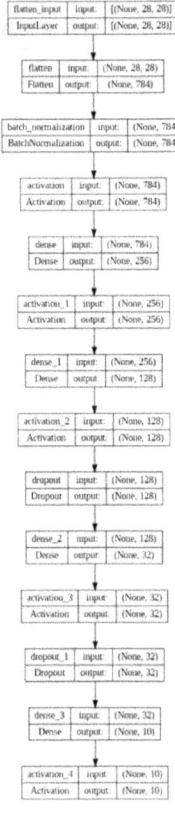

This is an illustration of a simple Artificial Neural Network (ANN) modeled by engineers. The model is used to demonstrate the complexities. Notice the various types of operations planned to train the ANN. This could be an initial design. Several iterations of testing various parameters and design decisions lead to the final ANN. Each round of testing could take few hours or days.

Training Neural Networks: The Heart of Learning

Training a neural network is akin to educating a mind. The goal is to imbue the network with the ability to make accurate predictions or decisions based on its inputs. This learning process is fundamentally about adjusting the network's internal parameters - the weights and biases - to minimize the difference between the network's predictions and the actual outcomes.

The Role of Backpropagation

Backpropagation is the cornerstone of neural network training. It is a method by which errors are propagated backward through the network. When a network makes a prediction, the discrepancy between this prediction and the true outcome (the error) is calculated. Backpropagation takes this error and distributes it back through the network's layers, providing a feedback mechanism that informs how the weights and biases should be adjusted.

This process involves complex calculus, specifically the computation of gradients that indicate how each weight and bias should be modified to reduce the overall error. Learning algorithms, most notably gradient descent, then use these gradients to update the network's parameters incrementally.

Iterative Learning and Optimization

The training process is iterative, involving multiple passes over the training dataset, during which the network's predictions are continually refined. With each iteration, the network edges closer to its optimal configuration, where the weights and biases are tuned to minimize prediction errors.

Regularization and Dropouts

Training a neural network is not without challenges. Issues such as overfitting, where the network becomes too attuned to the training data and performs poorly on unseen data, must be carefully managed. Regularization and dropout are employed to mitigate these risks, ensuring the network retains generality in its predictions.

Monitoring and Evaluation

The neural network's performance is closely monitored throughout the training process, often through a separate validation dataset that gauges the network's accuracy on data it hasn't seen during training. This monitoring helps identify when the network has reached its optimal state or is beginning to overfit.

Practical Implications for Managers

Understanding the principles of neural network architecture and training is crucial for managers venturing into deep learning. It provides insights into the complexities and considerations of developing effective neural network models. Managers need not delve into the mathematical intricacies but should grasp the strategic implications of network design choices and the training process.

Practical neural network projects hinge on a clear definition of the problem, thoughtful network design, meticulous data preparation, and vigilant monitoring during training. Managers are pivotal in steering these projects, ensuring alignment with business objectives, facilitating cross-disciplinary collaboration, and fostering an environment conducive to innovation and experimentation.

The architecture and training of neural networks encapsulate the essence of deep learning, offering a computational model capable of remarkable feats that parallel human intelligence in certain aspects. For managers, the journey into deep learning is not merely about adopting new technology but about embracing a new paradigm in data analysis and decision-making that can unlock unprecedented opportunities and drive transformative change within organizations.

Conclusion

For managers, the magic of neural networks lies not in their intricate mathematics but in their ability to learn from data and improve over time. Understanding the essential components and functions of ANNs provides a foundation for appreciating their potential in various applications, from customer behavior prediction and fraud detection to automation of routine tasks and beyond.

Deep learning projects driven by neural networks require careful planning, clear objectives, and collaboration across multidisciplinary teams. The manager's role is pivotal in aligning these projects with strategic business goals, ensuring ethical data use, and fostering an environment where innovation thrives.

As we delve deeper into the era of artificial intelligence, neural networks stand as a testament to human ingenuity, a bridge between the biological and the digital. For managers embarking on the journey of deep learning, the foundations of neural networks offer a starting point for transforming business practices, driving efficiency, and unlocking new opportunities in an increasingly data-driven world.

3. The Deep Learning Revolution

In the digital expanse, where innovation is constant, a revolution quietly unfolded, marking the beginning of what we now refer to as the Deep Learning Revolution. This chapter takes you through the transformative journey from traditional machine learning paradigms to the groundbreaking realm of deep learning, elucidating the pivotal breakthroughs and technological advancements that have catapulted deep learning to the vanguard of artificial intelligence.

From Roots to Revolution

The journey of deep learning from a conceptual framework to a transformative force in technology and business is fascinating and instructive. Its narrative spans several decades, marked by challenges, breakthroughs, and profound impacts across various sectors. This evolution is about technological advancement and is a testament to human ingenuity and persistence in pushing the boundaries of what machines can achieve.

The story begins in the mid-20th century with the development of the first artificial neural networks (ANNs). These early models were inspired by understanding the human brain's structure and function, specifically how neurons process and transmit information. The pioneers of ANNs envisioned creating machines capable of learning and making decisions, a revolutionary and ambitious concept given the time's technological constraints.

For decades, progress in neural networks was slow and fraught with challenges. The primary hurdles were the lack of computational power to process large datasets and the limited availability of such data. Early neural networks were simplistic, with only a few layers of neurons due to these constraints. They could perform basic tasks but were far from the complex functions their biological counterparts could manage.

The Convergence of Data and Computing Power

The turn of the millennium marked the beginning of a new era in computing and data. The advent of the Internet and the digitalization of information led to an exponential increase in data availability. Simultaneously, advances in semiconductor technology made computers faster, more powerful, and more affordable. This period also saw the development of Graphics Processing Units (GPUs), initially designed to render graphics for video games but soon proved exceptionally efficient at performing the matrix and vector operations central to neural network computation.

These technological advancements set the stage for the deep learning revolution. Researchers now had the tools to train more complex neural network models on much larger datasets, a critical factor in improving the models' accuracy and capabilities.

Landmark Moments in Deep Learning

One of the most significant milestones in the deep learning journey was the success of AlexNet in 2012. Named after Alex Krizhevsky, one of its creators, AlexNet was a deep neural network that competed in the ImageNet Large Scale Visual Recognition Challenge. This competition involved classifying images into thousands of categories, an incredibly challenging task for machines at the time.

AlexNet's victory was groundbreaking. It significantly outperformed all traditional machine learning algorithms, reducing the error rate substantially. This success didn't just win a competition; it demonstrated deep learning's unprecedented potential in processing and understanding complex visual data. AlexNet's architecture, particularly its convolutional layers, became a foundation for many subsequent models in image recognition and beyond.

The core of the deep learning revolution lies in developing and refining deep neural networks (DNNs). These networks feature multiple layers of neurons, or nodes, each layer capable of learning increasingly abstract data representations. This structure allows DNNs to learn complex patterns in large datasets, from the essential features in the initial layers to more intricate concepts in the deeper layers.

Unlike traditional machine learning models, which often require domain experts to identify and hand-engineer relevant features, DNNs learn these features directly from the data. This capability is crucial for tasks where the relevant features are not prominent or too complex for humans to codify, such as recognizing faces or understanding natural language.

The Democratization of Deep Learning

The democratization of deep learning signifies a transformative period in artificial intelligence, where advanced AI technologies have become accessible to a broad spectrum of users. The development and widespread adoption of open-source frameworks, the advent of cloud computing platforms, and a global shift towards collaborative innovation underpin this movement.

Open-Source Frameworks: The Catalysts of Democratization

The proliferation of open-source frameworks such as TensorFlow, developed by Google, and PyTorch, created by Facebook's AI Research lab, has been instrumental in democratizing deep learning. These frameworks offer a suite of tools, libraries, and community resources that significantly lower the barriers to entry for experimenting with and deploying deep learning models. They provide an abstraction layer over complex mathematical operations and hardware interactions, allowing both novice and seasoned practitioners to build and iterate on deep learning models without delving into the intricacies of underlying algorithms or optimization techniques.

The open-source nature of these frameworks fosters a culture of collaboration and innovation, where individuals and organizations worldwide contribute to the codebase, share best practices, and address common challenges. This collaborative ecosystem accelerates the pace of advancement in deep learning by making cutting-edge research and implementations readily available to the broader community.

Cloud Computing: Democratizing Access to Computational Resources

The advent of cloud computing has played a pivotal role in democratizing deep learning by making high-performance computing resources accessible to a broader audience. Cloud platforms like Amazon Web Services (AWS), Microsoft Azure, and Google Cloud Platform offer on-demand access to GPUs and TPUs (Tensor Processing Units), enabling individuals and organizations to train complex deep learning models without significant upfront investment in hardware.

Cloud computing also democratizes access to vast datasets and scalable storage solutions, crucial for training accurate and robust deep learning models. The pay-as-you-go cloud services model allows startups and individuals to leverage state-of-the-art computational resources and data storage facilities, leveling the playing field with more giant corporations.

The Challenges of Democratization

While the democratization of deep learning heralds numerous opportunities for innovation and advancement, it also introduces challenges that warrant careful consideration.

- **Data Bias and Fairness**: As deep learning models are trained on increasingly diverse datasets, the risk of perpetuating biases present in the data becomes a significant concern. Biased models can lead to unfair or discriminatory outcomes, particularly in sensitive applications such as hiring, lending, and law enforcement. Ensuring fairness and mitigating bias in AI systems is a critical challenge in the democratized landscape of deep learning.

- **Model Interpretability**: Deep learning models' complexity and "black box" nature pose challenges for interpretability and transparency. Understanding how these models make decisions is crucial for building trust in AI systems, especially in high-stakes domains such as healthcare and autonomous vehicles. Developing techniques for interpreting and explaining deep learning models is an ongoing area of research and an essential consideration for practitioners.
- **Environmental Impact**: Training large neural networks require significant computational resources, which, in turn, have a considerable environmental footprint due to energy consumption and associated carbon emissions. As deep learning becomes more widespread, addressing the environmental sustainability of training these models is an imperative challenge for the community.

The Role of Managers and Business Leaders

In the rapidly evolving digital landscape, managers and business leaders must understand, embrace, and strategically leverage the deep learning revolution. The democratization of deep learning presents opportunities for innovation and competitive advantage and necessitates a thoughtful approach to navigating its challenges.

- **Strategic Integration**: Managers must recognize the potential of deep learning to transform various facets of their business, from enhancing customer experiences and optimizing operations to developing new products and services. Strategic integration of deep learning technologies requires a clear vision, alignment with business objectives, and an understanding of AI's capabilities and limitations.
- **Ethical Considerations**: Business leaders play a crucial role in ensuring the ethical use of deep learning technologies. This involves addressing data privacy issues, ensuring fairness and transparency in AI systems, and

considering the broader societal implications of deploying these technologies.

- **Talent Development and Culture:** Fostering a culture of innovation and continuous learning is essential for organizations looking to thrive in the deep learning era. Internal talent development, investment in training and professional development, and promoting a culture of experimentation and collaboration are vital to building a skilled team capable of effectively leveraging deep learning technologies.
- **Navigating Challenges:** Managers must proactively address the challenges of democratizing deep learning. This includes implementing practices to mitigate data bias, investing in research and tools for model interpretability, and adopting sustainable practices to minimize the environmental impact of AI projects.

Impact Across Industries

The implications of the deep learning revolution extend far across the technological landscape. In healthcare, deep learning algorithms are now being used to diagnose diseases with accuracy that rivals or surpasses human experts. These algorithms can analyze medical images like X-rays and MRIs to detect anomalies like tumors or fractures.

In finance, deep learning is transforming customer service and fraud detection. Personalized banking services, such as chatbots and recommendation systems, are becoming more sophisticated, providing customers with tailored advice and services. Simultaneously, deep learning models detect unusual transaction patterns that may indicate fraudulent activity.

The automotive industry is undergoing a significant transformation with the development of autonomous vehicles. Deep learning enables these vehicles to understand and navigate their environment safely. It allows them to recognize objects, interpret road signs, and make complex driving decisions in real time.

The entertainment industry has also seen a profound impact from deep learning. Algorithms are now used in content recommendation systems, enhancing user experience by providing personalized content suggestions. Additionally, deep learning is revolutionizing content creation, with algorithms generating realistic computer-generated imagery (CGI) and even composing music.

The deep learning revolution is more than a series of technological advancements; it's a paradigm shift in how we approach problem-solving and innovation. Deep neural networks' ability to learn from vast amounts of data and perform tasks once deemed exclusive to human intelligence enhances existing applications and creates new possibilities.

As we continue to push the boundaries of what deep learning can achieve, it's essential to recognize the broader implications of these technologies. The deep learning revolution is reshaping industries, altering job landscapes, and even changing how we think about intelligence and creativity. It's enabling breakthroughs in science and medicine, making our cars safer and our online experiences more personalized. Yet, it raises important ethical and societal questions that need careful consideration, such as privacy concerns, potential bias in AI systems, and the impact on employment in specific sectors.

The transformative power of deep learning extends beyond mere technological innovation; it is a catalyst for a new era of discovery and understanding. This revolution offers unprecedented opportunities for managers and business leaders to innovate and compete in a rapidly evolving marketplace. Embracing deep learning can significantly improve operational efficiency, customer engagement, product development, and decision-making processes.

However, harnessing the full potential of deep learning requires more than just adopting new technologies. It demands a strategic approach to data management, a commitment to ethical AI practices, and an investment in talent development. Building teams with the right mix of skills and fostering a culture of continuous learning and innovation are critical for organizations aiming to leverage deep learning effectively.

As we look to the future, the pace of the deep learning revolution shows no signs of slowing down. Advances in neural network architectures, training methodologies, and hardware will continue to expand deep learning's capabilities and applications. We're also likely to see a greater emphasis on making AI systems more interpretable, transparent, and aligned with human values and ethics.

The deep learning revolution is not just about machines learning from data; it's about how we, as a society, learn to adapt, innovate, and thrive in an increasingly AI-driven world. For managers and business leaders, understanding the roots and implications of this revolution is the first step toward navigating its challenges and seizing the opportunities it presents. As we move forward, the key will be to leverage deep learning as a tool for business optimization and as a strategic asset that can drive sustainable growth, innovation, and competitive advantage in the digital age.

Conclusion

As we stand on the cusp of what might be the next chapter in this revolution, the future of deep learning seems boundless. The ongoing advancements in AI research promise even more sophisticated models and applications, potentially reshaping industries, economies, and societies in ways we are just beginning to comprehend.

In embracing the Deep Learning Revolution, leaders must leverage the technology for competitive advantage and guide its development and application with foresight and responsibility. The goal should be to ensure that deep learning serves humanity's broader interests, enhancing our capabilities without compromising our values or well-being.

As we navigate this complex landscape, collaboration, innovation, and ethical responsibility, principles must light our path. By doing so, we can harness the full potential of deep learning, transforming our businesses and industries and contributing positively to society and the world at large. The Deep Learning Revolution is not just a testament to human ingenuity and technological progress; it is a call to action for thoughtful, inclusive, and responsible leadership in the digital age.

4. Understanding Deep Learning Algorithms

In artificial intelligence, deep learning is a monumental achievement, pushing the boundaries of what machines can comprehend and accomplish. As managers and leaders in the modern business landscape, grasping the essence of deep learning algorithms is crucial, not for the intricate mathematical details but for their transformative potential and applications. This chapter demystifies the core algorithms that power deep learning, presenting them in a context that is accessible and relevant to management professionals.

Convolutional Neural Networks (CNNs): The Visionaries of AI

In the vast and intricate world of artificial intelligence, Convolutional Neural Networks (CNNs) stand out as a cornerstone of modern AI applications, particularly in image recognition and processing. Drawing inspiration from the human visual cortex, CNNs have revolutionized how machines interpret and understand visual data, from simple images to complex three-dimensional environments.

The Genesis of CNNs

The inception of CNNs was motivated by the quest to mimic the human brain's remarkable ability to recognize and categorize visual information quickly and precisely. The human visual cortex is adept at identifying patterns, shapes, and textures in the visual stimuli it receives, hierarchically processing this information to construct a coherent understanding of the scene. CNNs replicate this process through mathematical operations and layers that simulate the brain's neural networks, enabling machines to "see" and interpret images accurately.

The Architecture of CNNs

At the core of CNNs lies a unique architecture designed to learn spatial hierarchies of features automatically and efficiently from visual inputs. This architecture comprises several layers, each with a specific function.

- **Convolutional Layers**: These layers apply filters to the input images to create feature maps, highlighting essential features such as edges, textures, or specific shapes. The filters are adaptive, learning to capture the most relevant features for the task during the training process.
- **Pooling Layers**: Pooling, typically performed after convolution, reduces the dimensionality of the feature maps, making the network more efficient and less prone to overfitting. It retains the most critical information, such as the presence or absence of specific features in different image regions.
- **Fully Connected Layers**: Towards the end of the network, fully connected layers integrate the high-level features extracted by the previous layers to make final predictions or classifications. This is where the network combines all learned features to identify objects, diagnose diseases, or perform other specified tasks.

- **Activation Functions**: Interspersed within the network, activation functions introduce non-linearity, enabling the network to learn and represent complex patterns. The ReLU (Rectified Linear Unit) function is commonly used for its efficiency and effectiveness.

Applications of CNNs in Business

CNNs' practical applications are diverse and far-reaching. They impact numerous industries by enhancing efficiency, accuracy, and innovation.

- **Retail**: In the retail sector, CNNs can analyze in-store video footage to understand customer foot traffic, behavior, and product interactions. This data is invaluable for store managers seeking to optimize store layout, product placement, and inventory management, ultimately enhancing the shopping experience and increasing sales.
- **Manufacturing**: Quality control is paramount in manufacturing, and CNNs offer a powerful solution for automating defect detection in products on the assembly line. By recognizing

the characteristics of flawless and defective items, CNNs can inspect products with precision and consistency that surpasses human inspectors, reducing waste and ensuring product quality.
- **Healthcare**: One of the most profound applications of CNNs is in medical imaging, where they assist in diagnosing diseases from X-rays, MRIs, and other imaging technologies. CNNs can identify patterns indicative of various conditions, from fractures and tumors to more subtle signs of diseases like Alzheimer's, often with higher accuracy and speed than human radiologists.
- **Automotive**: In the automotive industry, CNNs are pivotal in developing autonomous vehicles. They enable cars to interpret and understand their surroundings, recognizing other vehicles, pedestrians, traffic signs, and lane markings, making real-time driving decisions that ensure safety and efficiency.

Overcoming Challenges with CNNs

Despite their impressive capabilities, deploying CNNs has challenges, particularly regarding data requirements and computational resources. CNNs require large amounts of labeled training data to learn effectively, which can be a significant hurdle in some applications. Additionally, training CNNs demands substantial computational power, often necessitating GPUs or cloud-based computing platforms.

Managers looking to implement CNN-based solutions must consider these factors, plan for data collection and annotation, and budget the necessary hardware or cloud services. Collaborating with data scientists and AI specialists is crucial to navigating these challenges and successfully integrating CNNs into business operations.

The Future of CNNs

The future of CNNs in business is vibrant and promising, with ongoing research and development continuously expanding their capabilities and applications. Advances in network architectures, training techniques, and hardware optimization are making CNNs more efficient, accurate, and accessible. As these technologies evolve, managers and business leaders have a unique opportunity to harness the power of CNNs, driving innovation, enhancing operational efficiency, and creating new value propositions in their respective industries.

As we look toward the future, the integration of CNNs within business operations will likely become more prevalent, driven by advancements in AI research, increased computational power, and the growing availability of big data. These developments will enable CNNs to tackle more complex tasks, open new avenues for innovation, and provide competitive advantages to early adopters.

However, effectively implementing CNNs in business contexts requires more than technical know-how. It demands a strategic approach that considers AI's ethical implications, ensures data privacy and security, and addresses the potential impacts on employment and skills requirements. Managers must foster a culture of continuous learning and adaptation, encouraging teams to explore CNNs' potential while remaining agile in the face of technological change.

Moreover, the democratization of AI tools, including user-friendly platforms and cloud services, is lowering the barriers to entry for businesses of all sizes to experiment with and deploy CNN-based solutions. This accessibility empowers managers to initiate pilot projects, validate use cases, and scale successful applications across their operations.

In embracing CNNs and other AI technologies, managers play a pivotal role in shaping the future of their organizations. By staying informed about the latest developments in deep learning, collaborating with experts in the field, and adopting a forward-thinking mindset, managers can navigate the complexities of the AI landscape. They can lead their organizations to harness the transformative power of CNNs, driving innovation, enhancing efficiency, and creating sustainable value in an increasingly digital and data-driven world.

In summary, Convolutional Neural Networks are a technological innovation and a strategic asset that can redefine business models, operational processes, and market competitiveness. As we venture deeper into the AI-driven era, the visionaries among us - those who can see beyond the horizon and embrace the potential of technologies like CNNs - will be the ones to lead their organizations to new heights of success and innovation.

Recurrent Neural Networks (RNNs): Masters of Sequence and Time

In the diverse landscape of artificial intelligence, Recurrent Neural Networks (RNNs) stand out for their unique ability to handle sequential data. This makes them indispensable for applications that require an understanding of time and order. Unlike their counterparts, RNNs possess a memory, allowing them to use information from previous inputs to inform future outputs.

The Core Mechanism of RNNs

At the heart of RNNs is their recursive structure, which allows for processing sequences of data. This is achieved by incorporating loops within the network, enabling information to persist across time steps. In practical terms, when an RNN processes a new piece of data, it combines this input with a 'memory' of what it has previously seen in the sequence. This feature enables RNNs to predict future events in a sequence based on the context of past events.

Key Applications of RNNs

Thanks to their ability to handle time-series data and sequences, RNNs have found applications across various fields. Some notable examples include the following.

- **Language Translation**: RNNs are at the forefront of natural language processing, particularly machine translation. They can understand the context and nuances of one language and translate it into another while maintaining the original meaning, tone, and style.
- **Speech Recognition**: In speech recognition, RNNs can process audio sequences, converting spoken words into text by analyzing the sound waves over time. This technology powers virtual assistants and voice-controlled devices, making human-machine interaction more seamless and intuitive.

- **Stock Market Prediction**: Financial analysts leverage RNNs to predict stock market trends by analyzing historical price data and identifying patterns that may indicate future movements. This predictive capability supports more informed investment strategies and risk management.
- **Customer Service Chatbots**: RNN-powered chatbots can engage in customer conversations, providing timely and contextually relevant support. These chatbots learn from past interactions, improving their ability to assist customers with various inquiries and tasks.

Advantages of RNNs in Business

The implementation of RNNs can offer several benefits to businesses. The most prominent ones are listed below.

- **Enhanced Decision-Making**: RNNs enable businesses to make more informed decisions by analyzing sequential data and predicting future events. This is particularly valuable in dynamic environments where past trends and patterns can inform future strategies.

- **Improved Customer Experience**: RNN-powered chatbots and virtual assistants can provide personalized, efficient customer service, increasing customer satisfaction and loyalty. These systems can simultaneously handle many inquiries, reducing wait times and operational costs.
- **Operational Efficiency**: In industries such as manufacturing and logistics, RNNs can forecast demand, optimize supply chain operations, and predict maintenance needs, thereby reducing downtime and improving efficiency.

Challenges and Considerations

While RNNs offer significant advantages, they also present challenges businesses must navigate.

- **Complexity and Resources**: RNNs can be complex to implement and require significant computational resources, especially for large datasets. Businesses must invest in the

necessary hardware or cloud services and have access to expertise in AI and machine learning.
- **Overfitting and Vanishing Gradients**: RNNs are susceptible to overfitting, where the model performs well on training data but poorly on new, unseen data. They can also suffer from vanishing gradients, a phenomenon where the network cannot learn from long-term dependencies in data. Addressing these issues requires careful model design and training.
- **Data Privacy and Security**: When deploying RNNs, especially in customer-facing applications, businesses must ensure the privacy and security of user data. Compliance with data protection regulations and implementing robust security measures are crucial.

The Future of RNNs

RNNs continue to evolve, with ongoing research focused on addressing their limitations and expanding their capabilities. Innovations such as Long-Short-Term Memory (LSTM) networks and Gated Recurrent

Units (GRUs) have significantly improved RNNs' ability to handle long-term dependencies in data.

As these technologies mature, we expect RNNs to play an increasingly central role in business applications, from enhancing predictive analytics and customer service to driving advancements in autonomous vehicles and personalized medicine. For managers and business leaders, staying abreast of these developments and understanding the potential of RNNs will be vital to leveraging their power to drive innovation and competitive advantage.

Integrating RNNs into business operations should be strategic and purpose-driven, focusing on areas where they can provide the most significant impact. Whether it's improving customer interactions through intelligent chatbots, enhancing financial forecasting models, optimizing supply chain logistics, or advancing healthcare diagnostics, RNNs offer a versatile and powerful tool for driving business value.

Looking ahead, the evolution of RNN technology and its applications is likely to accelerate, fueled by advances in AI research, increased computational power, and the exponential growth of data. Businesses that are proactive in exploring and adopting RNN-based solutions will be well-positioned to lead in innovation, offering superior products, services, and customer experiences.

In embracing the capabilities of Recurrent Neural Networks, managers and business leaders can transform their organizations, making them more agile, data-driven, and responsive to the challenges and opportunities of the digital age. The journey into the world of RNNs and AI, in general, is not without its challenges, but the potential rewards for businesses willing to navigate this landscape are immense. As we progress, RNNs will continue to be a key player in the unfolding story of AI in business, driving progress and innovation in an increasingly interconnected and data-rich world.

Autoencoders: The Art of Data Compression and Reconstruction

In the expansive domain of machine learning, autoencoders stand out for their unique ability to learn efficient data representations, compressing them into a more manageable form without significant information loss.

Understanding Autoencoders

Autoencoders are a type of neural network used in unsupervised learning, a branch of machine learning where models are trained without labeled outcomes. The primary function of an autoencoder is to learn a compressed, encoded representation of data and reconstruct it as closely as possible to its original form. This process of encoding and decoding serves as a means of data compression and enables the model to capture and prioritize the most salient features of the data.

The architecture of an autoencoder consists of two main components: the encoder and the decoder. The encoder compresses the input into a latent-space representation or a "code," which holds the compressed knowledge of the input data. The decoder then takes this code and reconstructs the input data as closely as possible. The performance of an autoencoder is often evaluated based on how well the reconstructed data matches the original input, with less emphasis on how the data is compressed in the latent space.

Applications of Autoencoders

Autoencoders have found applications across various domains, leveraging their ability to distill data into its most essential features. Some notable applications are as follows.

- **Data Denoising**: Autoencoders can effectively remove noise from data, making them invaluable in image and signal processing applications. By learning to ignore random noise, they can reconstruct cleaner versions of input data, enhancing the quality and usability of the data.
- **Dimensionality Reduction**: Similar to techniques like Principal Component Analysis (PCA), autoencoders can reduce the dimensionality of data, making it easier to process and analyze. This is particularly useful in fields like genomics and text mining, where high-dimensional data is expected.
- **Anomaly Detection**: One of the most impactful applications of autoencoders is identifying outliers or anomalies within datasets. By learning the typical patterns and features of data, autoencoders can highlight

instances that deviate significantly from the norm, signaling potential issues or areas of interest.

Autoencoders in Anomaly Detection

Autoencoders' ability to reconstruct data based on learned representations suits them for anomaly detection. In environments where data consistency is paramount, such as banking transactions or network traffic, any deviation from established patterns can indicate fraudulent or malicious activity.

- **Fraud Detection in Banking**: Autoencoders can sift through millions of banking transactions to learn what typical, legitimate transactions look like. When a transaction deviates significantly from this norm—perhaps in amount, frequency, or other transactional attributes—the autoencoder flags it as a potential fraud, prompting further investigation.
- **Cybersecurity**: In cybersecurity, autoencoders can analyze network traffic patterns, identifying unusual behavior that could indicate a breach or a cyber-attack. This

capability is crucial for maintaining the integrity and security of information systems, especially in an era where cyber threats are increasingly sophisticated.

Challenges and Considerations

While autoencoders offer significant advantages, their deployment is not without challenges. The data quality, the autoencoder's architecture, and the model's specific parameters are critical to its effectiveness and efficiency. Some considerations include the following.

- **Data Quality and Preprocessing**: An autoencoder's performance highly depends on the input data quality. Data preprocessing steps such as normalization, handling missing values, and feature selection are crucial to ensure the model learns meaningful representations.
- **Model Complexity**: The design of the autoencoder - such as the number of layers, the size of the latent space, and the activation functions used - must be carefully considered

to balance sufficient complexity to capture data patterns and the risk of overfitting.
- **Interpretability**: The latent space representations learned by an autoencoder can be challenging to interpret, making it difficult to understand what features the model considers essential. This lack of interpretability can be a hurdle in applications where understanding the model's decision-making process is critical.

The Future of Autoencoders

The field of autoencoders continues to evolve, with research focused on enhancing their capabilities and expanding their applications. Variants such as Variational Autoencoders (VAEs) and Conditional Autoencoders offer new avenues for exploration, including generative models and more controlled encoding processes.

As computational power increases and more sophisticated algorithms are developed, the potential applications of autoencoders in business and technology are set to expand. The possibilities are vast, from enhancing user experiences through personalized recommendations to improving operational efficiency by optimizing logistics and supply chains.

For managers and business leaders, understanding the capabilities and applications of autoencoders is essential for leveraging their potential to drive innovation and gain a competitive edge. By integrating autoencoders into their data analysis and processing workflows, businesses can unlock new insights, enhance decision-making, and improve their operations' efficiency and effectiveness.

Incorporating autoencoders requires a strategic approach. It starts with identifying the areas within the organization where their application can offer the most significant benefits. This could involve streamlining data processing, enhancing the accuracy of predictive models, or bolstering security measures against fraud and cyber threats.

Businesses must also invest in building or acquiring the necessary expertise to implement autoencoders successfully. This includes training existing staff on the fundamentals of autoencoders and their applications and potentially hiring specialists with deep knowledge of machine learning and neural networks.

Moreover, ethical considerations and data privacy concerns must be considered when deploying autoencoders, especially in sensitive areas such as customer data analysis and fraud detection. Businesses must ensure that their use of autoencoders complies with all relevant regulations and ethical guidelines, maintaining transparency and securing customer trust.

The role of autoencoders in business is set to grow, driven by the increasing availability of data and the continuous advancements in machine learning technologies. As autoencoders become more sophisticated and accessible, they will open new opportunities for businesses to innovate and optimize their operations across various industries.

Autoencoders represent a powerful tool in the arsenal of machine learning technologies, potentially transforming how businesses process and analyze data. By understanding the principles behind autoencoders, their practical applications, and the challenges associated with their deployment, managers and business leaders can harness this technology to enhance their operations, drive innovation, and secure a competitive advantage in the digital age. Embracing the capabilities of autoencoders is about adopting new technology and envisioning a future where data-driven insights lead to smarter decisions and more robust business outcomes.

Generative Adversarial Networks (GANs): The Creators of the AI World

Generative Adversarial Networks (GANs) stand out as one of the most innovative and transformative technologies in the vast expanse of artificial intelligence advancements. Introduced by Ian Goodfellow and his colleagues in 2014, GANs have swiftly ascended to prominence, captivating the imagination of researchers, artists, and entrepreneurs alike.

The Genesis of GANs

GANs represent a significant leap in generative models, primarily due to their novel structure and the adversarial process underpinning their training. A GAN consists of two neural networks: the Generator, which creates data, and the Discriminator, which evaluates the data. The generator aims to produce data so authentic that the discriminator cannot distinguish it from actual data. Conversely, the Discriminator becomes increasingly adept at detecting the Generator's fabrications. This dynamic rivalry improves the quality of the generated data, often resulting in outputs indistinguishable from genuine data.

Understanding the Adversarial Training Process

The adversarial training process is akin to a high-stakes game between the Generator and the Discriminator, each striving to outsmart the other. Initially, the generator produces data that is likely to be easily identified as fake. However, as training progresses, it learns from the Discriminator's feedback, refining its output to be more realistic. Simultaneously, the Discriminator enhances its ability to detect nuances that differentiate actual data from generated data. This iterative process continues until an equilibrium is reached, where the Generator's outputs are so convincing that the Discriminator's accuracy is akin to random guessing.

Applications of GANs in Various Industries

The implications of GANs extend far beyond the theoretical or academic realms, touching upon numerous practical applications across diverse sectors.

- **Entertainment and Media**: GANs have revolutionized content creation in the entertainment industry, particularly in visual effects and virtual environment generation. Film producers and game developers can use GANs to create hyper-realistic scenes and characters, reducing the need for costly physical sets or extensive manual labor in animation. This cuts production costs and opens new creative possibilities that were previously unfeasible.
- **Product Design and Manufacturing**: GANs are invaluable in product design, offering a way to generate and iterate on design prototypes

rapidly. Designers can input initial design parameters into a GAN, producing a range of variations. This accelerates the creative process, enabling teams to explore a broader spectrum of design options and efficiently identify optimal solutions.

- **Fashion and Art**: The fashion industry has embraced GANs for creating innovative patterns and designs, while artists use them to push the boundaries of creativity, generating artworks that blend styles from different eras or creating entirely new aesthetics. GANs enable collaborative creativity between humans and machines, leading to unprecedented forms of expression.
- **Drug Discovery and Healthcare**: GANs are being explored for their potential in drug discovery and personalized medicine in healthcare and pharmaceuticals. GANs can help identify new compounds with desired therapeutic properties by generating molecular structures, significantly speeding up drug development.

Ethical Considerations and Challenges

While GANs offer tremendous potential, their capabilities also present ethical challenges, particularly concerning generating deepfakes and disseminating misinformation. Deepfakes are hyper-realistic videos or audio recordings generated by GANs, which can convincingly depict individuals saying or doing things they never did. This poses significant risks regarding privacy, security, and the integrity of information, necessitating the development of ethical guidelines and detection tools to mitigate misuse.

Furthermore, training GANs require substantial computational resources and data, which can be prohibitive for smaller organizations or individual researchers. Ensuring fair access to these technologies and the benefits they can provide is an ongoing challenge within the AI community.

The Future of GANs

Looking ahead, the trajectory of GANs appears boundless, with continuous advancements expanding their capabilities and applications. Future iterations of

GANs may offer even more efficiency, versatility, and accessibility, enabling broader adoption across industries. As GANs become more integrated into various sectors, understanding their potential and limitations will be crucial for managers and leaders aiming to leverage these technologies for innovation and competitive advantage.

Generative Adversarial Networks have ushered in a new era in artificial intelligence, characterized by creating remarkably realistic data. From transforming content creation in entertainment to accelerating innovation in product design and drug discovery, GANs have demonstrated their vast potential to reshape industries. However, navigating the ethical landscape and ensuring the responsible use of GANs remains paramount. As we venture further into the AI-driven future, the role of GANs will undoubtedly continue to evolve, pushing the boundaries of what is possible with artificial intelligence. The onus falls on business leaders, technologists, and policymakers alike to harness the power of GANs responsibly, fostering innovation while safeguarding against potential misuse.

For managers and decision-makers, the advent of GAN technology presents both an opportunity and a challenge. The opportunity lies in the ability to drive unprecedented creativity, efficiency, and personalization in products and services. The challenge, however, is to remain vigilant about the ethical implications of this technology, ensuring that its deployment enhances societal values and does not undermine them.

As GANs become more sophisticated, we may see new regulatory frameworks emerging to ensure the ethical use of AI. These frameworks will likely focus on transparency, accountability, and the prevention of harm, guiding businesses in the responsible deployment of GANs. Moreover, public awareness and understanding of GANs will be crucial in shaping a societal consensus on the acceptable use of this technology.

In the realm of business strategy, GANs can be a double-edged sword. On the one hand, they offer the potential to leapfrog competitors through innovation; on the other hand, they necessitate reevaluating traditional business models as the lines between digital and physical realities blur. Strategic foresight and adaptability will be vital in navigating this shifting landscape, focusing on building capabilities to integrate GANs into businesses' value propositions.

Future developments in GAN technology may also lead to new partnerships and collaborations between businesses, researchers, and regulatory bodies. These collaborations could foster an ecosystem that drives technological advancement and ensures that such advancements contribute positively to society.

By embracing GANs, businesses have the potential to redefine their industries, creating experiences and solutions that were previously unimaginable. However, this journey must be underpinned by a commitment to ethical principles and a deep understanding of technology's impact. As we stand on the cusp of this new frontier in AI, the choices made by today's leaders will shape the trajectory of GANs and their role in our collective future.

Conclusion

Understanding these algorithms' core concepts and potential applications empowers managers to envision their practical utility in various business contexts. The key lies in recognizing the problem at hand and matching it with the appropriate deep-learning solution. Whether enhancing customer experiences, streamlining operations or driving innovation, deep learning algorithms offer a toolkit for tackling complex challenges with newfound agility and insight.

As we delve deeper into the era of artificial intelligence, managers' role in harnessing the power of deep learning becomes increasingly pivotal. By fostering a culture of innovation, continuous learning, and ethical AI use, managers can lead their teams and organizations to thrive in this transformative landscape. The journey through deep learning algorithms is about understanding technology and envisioning a future where AI and human ingenuity converge to create unprecedented value and opportunities.

5. Deep Learning in Practice

Deep learning, a subset of machine learning inspired by the structure and function of the human brain, has transformed how businesses leverage data, automate processes, and innovate products and services. In this chapter, we delve into the practical aspects of implementing deep learning projects, guiding managers through data collection, model selection, training, and evaluation while addressing common challenges that may arise.

Initiating a Deep Learning Project

Initiating a deep learning project is a strategic endeavor that requires careful planning, a clear vision, and a deep understanding of the organization's goals and challenges. At the core of this process is articulating the problem to be solved or the opportunity to be seized. This foundational step is crucial, as it sets the direction for the entire project and ensures that deploying deep learning technologies aligns with the organization's broader objectives.

For managers embarking on this journey, the first task is to conduct a comprehensive assessment of the organization's operations, services, and products to identify potential areas for improvement or innovation through deep learning. This exploration involves engaging with various stakeholders across departments to gather insights into the pain points, inefficiencies, and bottlenecks that could be addressed with AI solutions. For instance, in customer service, AI chatbots powered by deep learning can handle many inquiries in real-time, reducing wait times and freeing human agents to tackle more complex issues. In manufacturing, deep learning can be applied to predictive maintenance, analyzing data from machinery to predict failures before they occur, minimizing downtime, and reducing repair costs.

Once potential applications have been identified, managers must define specific, measurable objectives for the deep learning project. This might involve setting targets for reducing customer service response times, improving demand forecasting accuracy, or achieving a specific percentage reduction in equipment failures. Clear objectives provide a benchmark for success and help prioritize projects based on their potential impact and feasibility.

The next step involves a feasibility assessment, where managers must consider the availability of data, the required computational resources, and the expertise needed to develop and deploy deep learning models. This stage may reveal the need for data collection initiatives, investments in hardware or cloud computing services, or the recruitment of skilled personnel.

Engaging with data science and AI experts is crucial at this stage to understand what deep learning can and cannot achieve. These experts can provide valuable insights into the latest advancements in AI, the limitations of current technologies, and the types of problems most amenable to deep learning solutions.

Managers can build a detailed project plan with a clear problem definition, set objectives, and a feasibility assessment. This plan should outline the data collection and preparation steps, model development and training, implementation, and evaluation. It should also include timelines, resource allocations, and risk management strategies.

In summary, initiating a deep learning project is a multi-faceted process that requires managers to blend strategic insight with technical understanding. By clearly defining the problem and objectives, assessing feasibility, and engaging with experts, managers can lay a solid foundation for successful deep learning initiatives that drive value, enhance efficiency, and foster innovation within their organizations.

Data Collection and Preparation

Embarking on a deep learning project is akin to laying the foundation for a skyscraper. Just as the strength of a building lies in its foundation, the success of a deep learning model hinges on the quality, quantity, and relevance of the data it's trained on.

Data Collection: Casting a Wide Net

Data collection is the first step in a deep learning project's journey. It involves gathering information from many sources to feed into the model. This stage is crucial because the data is the raw material from which the model learns and derives insights. Managers are pivotal in ensuring the collected data is abundant and pertinent to the problem.

- **Diverse Sources**: Data can come from internal databases, capturing years of organizational operations, customer interactions, or product performances. External sources, such as online repositories or public datasets, can complement this internal data, offering broader perspectives or additional insights. Real-time data streams, especially in IoT (Internet of Things) applications or social media analytics, provide a continuous influx of fresh data, enriching the model's learning potential.
- **Quality over Quantity**: While the volume of data is essential, its quality is paramount. High-quality data is accurate, complete, and relevant. Ensuring data quality might involve verifying the accuracy of the data sources, checking for completeness, and assessing the data's applicability to the specific deep-learning task.
- **Representativeness and Bias**: The data must represent the problem space well, covering all

scenarios the model might encounter post-deployment. It is also crucial to scrutinize the data for biases that could skew the model's learning, leading to flawed outputs. Managers must champion diversity and inclusivity in data collection to mitigate these risks.

Data Preparation: The Art of Refinement

Once collected, raw data is rarely ready for model training. It often contains inconsistencies, anomalies, or irrelevant information that could impair the model's learning process. Data preparation, therefore, becomes an essential endeavor to transform raw data into a clean, organized format conducive to deep learning.

- **Data Cleaning**: This process involves identifying and correcting errors or inaccuracies in the data. It might include filling in missing values, correcting typos or mislabelings, and addressing duplicate entries. The goal is to ensure that the data fed into the model is as accurate and complete as possible.

- **Normalization and Standardization**: Deep learning models often perform better when numerical data values are on a similar scale. Normalization (rescaling the data to a [0, 1] range) and standardization (reshaping the data to have a mean of 0 and a standard deviation of 1) are common techniques to achieve this. These processes help speed up the model's convergence and improve its performance.
- **Feature Engineering**: This involves transforming raw data into a set of features that the model can understand. It might include extracting relevant information from text, aggregating data points, or creating new variables from existing ones. Practical feature engineering can significantly enhance the model's learning capability.
- **Data Augmentation**: In cases where data is scarce or unbalanced, data augmentation can be employed to expand the dataset artificially. This is common in image processing tasks, where images can be rotated, flipped, or cropped to create additional training examples.
- **Partitioning**: Finally, the prepared data is divided into subsets, typically for training,

validation, and testing. This partitioning is critical for evaluating the model's performance on unseen data, ensuring its generalizability and robustness.

Collaboration with Data Scientists

Managers might not delve into the technical minutiae of data preparation, but their role in facilitating collaboration with data scientists is indispensable. They must ensure that the objectives of the deep learning project are communicated and that the data preparation strategies align with these goals. By fostering a cooperative environment, managers can bridge the gap between business needs and technical execution, steering the project toward success.

Choosing the Right Algorithm

Choosing the suitable algorithm is a pivotal step in the journey of a deep learning project, akin to selecting the appropriate tool for a job. The landscape of deep learning is replete with many algorithms, each with its strengths, weaknesses, and quirks. For managers steering deep learning initiatives, making an informed choice about which algorithm to employ can significantly impact the project's outcome. This decision-making process hinges on understanding the nature of the problem and matching it with an algorithm designed to tackle similar challenges.

Understanding the Problem Space

The first step in selecting an algorithm is delineating the problem space. Is the task at hand about recognizing patterns in images, understanding sequences in text or time-series data, or generating new data that mimics a particular distribution? For instance, tasks involving image recognition, object detection, or segmentation naturally lean towards Convolutional Neural Networks (CNNs) due to their proficiency in handling spatial hierarchies in visual data.

Conversely, if the problem involves sequences or time-dependent data - such as language translation, stock market prediction, or sentiment analysis from the text - Recurrent Neural Networks (RNNs) and their more advanced variants like LSTM (Long Short-Term Memory) networks become prime candidates. Their architecture, designed to process data sequentially and remember past inputs, suits them, particularly for these tasks.

In scenarios where the goal is to generate new data that is indistinguishable from actual data - be it images, text, or even music - Generative Adversarial Networks (GANs) stand out. Their unique structure, comprising a generator and a discriminator in a competitive setup, enables them to produce highly realistic outputs, opening avenues in content creation, design, and even scientific research.

Matching Algorithms with Applications

Once the nature of the problem is understood, the next step involves matching it with an algorithm known for its effectiveness in similar applications. This requires managers to have a broad understanding of the typical applications of various deep-learning algorithms.

- **CNNs**: Beyond image processing, CNNs are also adept at tasks like anomaly detection in visual quality control systems in

manufacturing or analyzing medical imagery for diagnostic purposes.
- **RNNs**: These are not limited to text or speech; they're also effective in predictive maintenance by analyzing time-series sensor data from machinery to predict failures.
- **GANs**: While known for generating realistic images, GANs are also used in data augmentation, especially in fields where data is scarce or expensive to obtain, enhancing the robustness of other models trained on the augmented dataset.

Considering Limitations and Practicalities

Every algorithm comes with its limitations and requirements. For instance, CNNs might require substantial amounts of labeled image data for training. At the same time, RNNs might suffer from issues like vanishing gradients, especially when dealing with long sequences, making training challenging.

Practical considerations also play a crucial role in the selection process. The availability of computational resources, the size and diversity of the dataset, and even the project's timeline can influence the choice of algorithm. Advanced models like GANs necessitate significant computational power and expertise to train effectively, which could be a limiting factor for some projects.

Moreover, the dynamic nature of the AI field means that new algorithms and improvements are continually emerging. Staying abreast of the latest developments can give managers additional options and insights, enabling more informed decision-making.

For managers, fostering a collaborative environment where insights from data scientists, domain experts, and IT professionals converge can facilitate this decision-making process. By aligning the choice of algorithm with the project's objectives and constraints, managers can set the stage for successful deep-learning implementations that drive value and innovation.

Model Training and Fine-Tuning

Bringing a deep learning model to fruition involves two critical phases: training and fine-tuning. This process is akin to teaching children to understand the world around them, with training introducing the basics and fine-tuning to refine their understanding to a more nuanced level. For managers overseeing deep learning projects, navigating these phases efficiently is pivotal to achieving a model that learns effectively and aligns with the project's objectives and constraints.

The Training Phase

Training a deep learning model is the core phase where the model learns from data. This is where the mathematical architecture of the model, designed to mimic the human brain's learning process, is tested. The model is exposed to vast amounts of data, learning to recognize patterns, make connections, and derive insights that enable it to perform tasks such as prediction, classification, or recognition.

One of the most significant considerations during this phase is allocating **computational resources**. Deep learning models require substantial computational power, particularly those dealing with large datasets or complex architectures like CNNs or RNNs. GPUs (Graphics Processing Units) have become the de facto standard for training deep learning models because they efficiently perform parallel operations on large datasets. Cloud-based platforms offer scalable solutions for projects with limited in-house resources, allowing managers to access high-performance computing resources on demand, aligning with the project's scale and budgetary constraints.

Training involves feeding the prepared data into the model in batches and iteratively adjusting the model's internal parameters based on its performance. This process is guided by a loss function, quantifying the difference between the model's predictions and the actual outcomes. The goal is to minimize this loss, indicating that the model's predictions are becoming increasingly accurate. This iterative process, often running for thousands or even millions of iterations, is where the bulk of computational resources are consumed.

The Fine-Tuning Phase

Once the initial training is complete, the model enters the fine-tuning phase. This phase is crucial for refining the model's performance, making it more aligned with the specific nuances of its designed task.

Hyperparameters are the settings that define the model's architecture and training process, such as the learning rate, batch size, or the number of layers in the neural network. Unlike the model's internal parameters, learned from the data, hyperparameters are set before training begins, significantly influencing the model's learning efficiency and performance.

Fine-tuning involves adjusting these hyperparameters based on the model's performance on a validation set - a portion of the data not seen by the model during training. This process requires a delicate balance. Setting the learning rate too low might make the training unnecessarily long and prone to getting stuck in local minima. At the same time, a too high rate might cause the model to overshoot the optimal solution.

The fine-tuning phase also involves continuous validation of the model's performance. This is typically done using a separate dataset that was not used during the initial training. The model's predictions are compared against actual outcomes, providing insights into its accuracy and generalizability.

This phase might reveal that certain aspects of the model require adjustment - perhaps the architecture needs to be deeper to capture more complex patterns, or the data needs to be augmented to provide a more comprehensive learning base. This leads to an iterative refinement process, where adjustments are made, and the model is retrained and re-evaluated until the desired performance is achieved.

Challenges and Considerations

Model training and fine-tuning are not without challenges. Overfitting is a common issue where the model performs well on the training data but poorly on new, unseen data. Regularization techniques, dropout layers in neural networks, or acquiring more diverse training data can mitigate this.

Another challenge is the computational cost, both in terms of time and resources. Efficient resource allocation, parallel processing, and leveraging cloud-based solutions can help manage these costs.

Training and fine-tuning a deep learning model are complex, resource-intensive processes that require a strategic approach. For managers, this means allocating resources judiciously and fostering a culture of experimentation and patience. By carefully navigating the training and fine-tuning phases, managers can guide their teams toward developing robust, effective deep-learning models that drive innovation and value within their organizations.

Evaluating Model Performance

In deep learning, the development phase doesn't conclude with the model's training. A pivotal step that follows is model evaluation - a rigorous process that determines the model's effectiveness and readiness for deployment. This step is akin to a final exam for the model, testing its learned knowledge against new, unseen data to ensure it performs as expected in real-world scenarios.

Testing on Unseen Data

The cornerstone of model evaluation is testing the model on a dataset it hasn't encountered during training. This unseen data is a proxy for real-world data, providing an objective basis for assessing the model's generalizability and performance. The rationale is straightforward: a model that performs well on new data will likely deliver reliable results when deployed in actual applications, from customer service bots to predictive maintenance systems.

Choosing Relevant Metrics

The metrics chosen to evaluate a model's performance are crucial and must align with the project's objectives and the nature of the task. Standard metrics include the following.

- **Accuracy**: This metric is often used for classification tasks and represents the proportion of correct predictions made by the model out of all predictions. While intuitive, accuracy might not be suitable for imbalanced datasets where correctly identifying a rare class is more critical.
- **Precision and Recall**: Precision measures the proportion of correct identifications, while recall measures the proportion of actual positives that were correctly identified. These metrics are particularly relevant in scenarios where the costs of false positives or false negatives are high, such as spam detection or medical diagnoses.

- **F1 Score**: The F1 score harmonizes precision and recall into a single metric, providing a balanced view of the model's performance, especially in imbalanced datasets.

Setting Performance Benchmarks

Managers play a crucial role in defining success for a deep learning project. This involves setting performance benchmarks the model must achieve to be ready for deployment. These benchmarks should be ambitious yet realistic, reflecting the model's intended use case and the level of performance required to add value or solve the problem at hand.

For instance, a model designed to detect fraudulent transactions might require extremely high precision to minimize false positives, which could lead to customer dissatisfaction. Conversely, a model for identifying potential leads in a marketing database might prioritize recall, ensuring that no potential leads are missed, even at the cost of some false positives.

Deciding on Acceptable Thresholds

Beyond choosing metrics and setting benchmarks, managers must also decide on acceptable thresholds for these metrics. This decision is often a balancing act, weighing the model's performance against operational considerations like the cost of errors, the model's impact on user experience, and the feasibility of achieving higher performance given the available data and resources.

Iterative Improvement

Model evaluation is rarely a one-off process. It's common for initial evaluations to reveal areas where the model falls short of the benchmarks. In such cases, the model may need to be retrained with additional data, fine-tuned with adjusted hyperparameters, or even restructured in terms of architecture. This iterative evaluation, adjustment, and re-evaluation process is essential for honing the model's performance to meet the project's objectives.

Addressing Common Challenges

Navigating the complex terrain of deep learning projects involves confronting challenges that can impede progress and impact outcomes. Understanding these challenges and devising strategic solutions is essential for managers at the helm of these initiatives to steer projects toward success.

Data Privacy and Security

In the data-driven world of deep learning, privacy and security concerns are paramount, especially when personal or sensitive information is involved. Data collection, storage, and processing must be handled with the utmost care to protect individual privacy rights and comply with stringent regulations like the General Data Protection Regulation (GDPR) in the European Union.

Solutions
Data Anonymization and Pseudonymization: Implementing techniques to remove or mask personal identifiers from data sets can help mitigate

privacy risks, making it difficult to link data back to individuals.
Encryption: Encrypting data at rest and in transit ensures that the information remains secure and indecipherable to unauthorized parties even if data breaches occur.
Compliance Audits: Regular audits and assessments can help ensure data handling practices comply with relevant laws and regulations, safeguarding against legal and reputational risks.

Resource Allocation

Deep learning models, known for their depth and complexity, demand significant computational power for training, often necessitating Graphics Processing Units (GPUs) or even more advanced hardware. The cost and availability of these resources can pose substantial challenges, particularly for large-scale projects or organizations with limited budgets.

Solutions
Cloud Computing: Leveraging cloud-based platforms can provide scalable, on-demand access to computational resources, allowing managers to adjust usage based on the project's phase and needs, optimizing costs.
Efficient Model Design: Working with data scientists to design efficient models regarding computational requirements without compromising performance can help alleviate resource constraints.
Resource Prioritization: Allocating resources strategically to different phases of the project, prioritizing critical tasks, and scheduling less resource-intensive tasks during off-peak hours can optimize usage and costs.

Managing Project Timelines

The inherently experimental nature of deep learning, particularly during the model training and fine-tuning phases, can make project timelines unpredictable. This unpredictability can complicate planning and resource allocation, potentially leading to delays and budget overruns.

Solutions
Agile Methodologies: Adopting an agile approach, characterized by iterative development and regular evaluations, can enhance flexibility, allowing teams to adapt to unforeseen challenges and changes in project scope or direction.
Milestone-Based Planning: Setting clear milestones and checkpoints throughout the project can help track progress and identify potential delays early, allowing for timely interventions.
Contingency Planning: Building contingencies into project plans, both in terms of time and resources, can provide a buffer against unforeseen delays, reducing the risk of significant disruptions.

Fostering a Collaborative and Continuous Learning Environment

Deep learning projects' dynamic and complex nature necessitates a synergistic approach, where collaboration and continuous learning are encouraged and ingrained in the organizational culture. The convergence of diverse expertise - from data scientists and domain experts to IT professionals - creates a fertile ground for innovation, ensuring that deep learning initiatives are technically sound and closely aligned with business objectives.

Building a Collaborative Framework

Collaboration is the linchpin of success in deep learning projects. The intricate interplay between various aspects of these projects - data preparation, algorithm selection, model training, and deployment - requires a seamless exchange of ideas and information across different teams.

Cross-functional Teams

Establishing cross-functional teams is a strategic approach to foster collaboration. By bringing together professionals from various disciplines, organizations can ensure a holistic view of the project, where technical challenges are addressed with a keen eye on business implications. Data scientists bring their expertise in algorithms and model training, domain experts contribute with a nuanced understanding of the field, and IT professionals ensure the robustness of the underlying infrastructure.

Regular Sync-ups and Knowledge Sharing

Regular meetings and knowledge-sharing sessions are vital to keep all team members on the same page. These forums allow for exchanging ideas, progress updates, and brainstorming solutions to emerging challenges. They also serve as platforms for domain experts to elucidate nuanced aspects of the problem, enabling data scientists to tailor models more effectively.

Cultivating a Culture of Continuous Learning

The field of deep learning is in a state of constant evolution, with new research, techniques, and best practices emerging regularly. Staying competitive necessitates an organizational culture that values and promotes continuous learning.

Professional Development Opportunities

Providing team members with opportunities for professional development - be it workshops, conferences, online courses, or certifications - enables them to hone their skills and stay abreast of the latest advancements in the field. This benefits the individual's career trajectory and enhances the team's collective capability to tackle complex deep-learning projects.

Learning from Projects

Each deep learning project, with its unique set of challenges and learnings, serves as a valuable knowledge resource. Encouraging teams to document their experiences, successes, and failures and to share these insights across the organization can transform individual projects into collective learning experiences. This knowledge repository becomes invaluable, guiding future projects and sparking innovation.

Embracing Failure as a Learning Opportunity

In the experimental realm of deep learning, not every initiative will meet its objectives. Cultivating an environment where failure is viewed as an integral part of the learning process is crucial. Encouraging teams to dissect failed projects to understand what went wrong - and, more importantly, why - can provide critical insights that inform future strategies and prevent repeating the same mistakes.

Conclusion

The success of deep learning projects hinges not just on the algorithms' sophistication or the data quality but equally on the collaborative synergy among the teams involved and their commitment to continuous learning. By fostering a collaborative environment and nurturing a culture that values continuous learning and innovation, organizations can harness the full potential of deep learning to drive competitive advantage and achieve breakthrough outcomes.

Implementing deep learning in practice requires a strategic approach, from defining the project's goals to evaluating the model's performance. Managers are crucial in steering these projects toward success, ensuring that the technical aspects are aligned with business objectives, and navigating the challenges that arise. By embracing deep learning, managers can unlock new opportunities for innovation, efficiency, and competitive advantage, transforming their organizations in the digital era.

6. Applications of Deep Learning in Business

Deep learning has transcended its academic origins to become a pivotal force in business innovation. Across industries, companies harness their power to solve complex problems, enhance customer experiences, and gain a competitive edge. This chapter delves into the diverse applications of deep learning in business, illustrating its transformative impact through real-world case studies.

Finance: Revolutionizing Risk Management and Fraud Detection

Deep learning has profoundly transformed the finance sector, particularly in risk management and fraud detection. Traditional methods, while effective to a certain extent, often lack the dynamism and depth required to parse through and make sense of the increasingly complex financial data. Deep learning, with its ability to learn from data in a more human-like manner, provides more accurate and significantly more efficient solutions.

The application of deep learning in finance is multifaceted, ranging from enhancing customer service through chatbots to predicting market trends. However, its impact is particularly notable in risk management and fraud detection. Here, deep learning algorithms sift through massive datasets, identifying complex patterns and anomalies that could indicate fraudulent activities or financial risks that are not immediately apparent.

Case Study: Fintech Startup Enhances Loan Processing with RNNs

A Fintech startup aiming to disrupt the traditional loan processing model turned to deep learning to refine its risk assessment process. The goal was to move beyond the conventional credit scoring systems that primarily rely on credit history, income, and employment status.

> **Challenge**: Traditional loan processing methods often overlook nuanced behavioral patterns that could indicate a borrower's reliability. Additionally,

they tend to be rigid, not accounting for many personal circumstances affecting borrowers' ability to pay.

Solution: The startup employed Recurrent Neural Networks (RNNs), a class of deep learning models adept at handling sequential data, to analyze applicants' financial transactions over time. RNNs, with their ability to 'remember' previous inputs, were ideal for discerning patterns in how individuals manage their finances over extended periods.

Moreover, the model incorporated non-traditional data points, including social media activity and online behavior, to gauge lifestyle and spending habits. This holistic view allowed for a more nuanced risk assessment beyond what traditional credit scores could offer.

Outcome: The RNN model significantly outperformed traditional risk assessment methods, reducing default rates by a notable margin. The startup could offer more personalized loan products, adjusting terms based on individual risk profiles. This enhanced customer satisfaction and attracted a broader clientele, including those whom

> conventional banks might overlook due to a lack of extensive credit history.

Impact and Implications

This case study underscores the transformative potential of deep learning in the finance sector. By leveraging RNNs, the fintech startup could tap into a wealth of data, gaining previously inaccessible insights. This approach to risk assessment is more inclusive, considering a more comprehensive array of factors that influence financial behavior.

Broader Applications in Finance

The success of this fintech startup exemplifies a broader trend in finance where deep learning is being employed.

- **Enhance Fraud Detection**: Deep learning models are trained to recognize fraudulent transactions by learning from historical fraud patterns. They can adapt to new tactics employed by fraudsters, staying one step ahead.

- **Improve Customer Profiling**: Deep learning models can segment customers more accurately by analyzing transaction data, leading to personalized financial products and services.
- **Optimize Trading Strategies**: In stock trading, deep learning algorithms can analyze market data to predict trends, providing traders with insights to inform their strategies.

Challenges and Considerations

While the benefits are substantial, deploying deep learning in finance is not devoid of challenges. Data privacy is a primary concern, especially when personal and financial data are involved. Ensuring compliance with regulations like GDPR is paramount. Additionally, the black-box nature of deep learning models poses transparency issues, making it crucial to develop interpretable models, especially in a sector as regulated as finance.

Healthcare: Enhancing Diagnostics and Personalizing Treatment

Deep learning's incursion into healthcare marks a paradigm shift in diagnostics and personalized treatment. The capability of Convolutional Neural Networks (CNNs) to interpret complex medical images and other biomedical data is paving the way for earlier, more accurate diagnoses and tailored treatment strategies, thereby significantly enhancing patient care and outcomes.

The application of deep learning in healthcare is broad and impactful, encompassing areas such as disease detection, genetic analysis, and the development of personalized treatment plans. CNNs are instrumental in analyzing medical imagery, such as MRIs, CT scans, and X-rays, allowing for identifying disease markers that may be invisible to the human eye.

Case Study 1: Early Detection of Melanoma through CNNs

A leading dermatology research center employed deep learning to improve the early detection of melanoma, a deadly skin cancer.

Challenge: The challenge was the subtle presentation of melanoma in its early stages, which often leads to misdiagnosis.
Solution: The center developed a CNN model trained on thousands of high-resolution images of various skin lesions. By learning from patterns associated with malignant and benign lesions, CNN could distinguish between them with remarkable accuracy.
Outcome: The deep learning model achieved a diagnostic accuracy comparable to and sometimes surpassing experienced dermatologists. This tool has become an invaluable aid in clinics, significantly improving early detection rates of melanoma and, by extension, patient survival rates.

Case Study 2: Predicting Alzheimer's Disease Progression

A neurology institute focused on Alzheimer's research integrated deep learning to predict the progression of the disease, a crucial aspect of patient care planning and treatment adjustment.

Challenge: Alzheimer's disease progression can vary significantly among patients, making standardized treatment plans less effective. Early and accurate prediction of disease progression is essential for timely intervention.
Solution: The institute utilized a deep learning model to analyze patient data, including brain scans, genetic information, and cognitive test results. The model identified patterns and correlations that could predict individual patients' disease trajectories.
Outcome: The deep learning model provided predictions with a high degree of accuracy, enabling clinicians to tailor treatment and care plans more precisely to the patient's predicted disease progression, thereby improving the quality of life for patients and their families.

Case Study 3: Personalizing Cancer Treatment

A renowned medical research institution developed a deep learning algorithm that revolutionized cancer treatment by personalizing it to the genetic makeup of individual patients.

Challenge: Cancer treatment often follows a one-size-fits-all approach despite the disease's known genetic variability. This can lead to ineffective treatments for certain patients, necessitating a more personalized approach.
Solution: The institution employed a deep learning algorithm that analyzed genetic data from tumor biopsies and medical imaging to identify each patient's most effective treatment options. The algorithm considered various factors to predict treatment efficacy, including genetic mutations, tumor size, and location.
Outcome: The personalized treatment plans significantly improved patient outcomes, with higher remission rates and fewer side effects. This approach's success has led to its adoption in oncology departments worldwide, marking a significant advancement in cancer treatment.

Impact and Implications

These case studies illustrate the profound impact deep learning has on healthcare, particularly in diagnostics and personalized treatment. By leveraging the pattern recognition capabilities of CNNs and other deep learning models, medical professionals can detect diseases earlier and more accurately, leading to more effective interventions.

Moreover, the ability to personalize treatment plans based on a patient's unique genetic profile represents a significant leap forward in precision medicine. This improves treatment efficacy and minimizes the risk of adverse reactions, enhancing overall patient care.

Challenges and Considerations

Despite these advancements, integrating deep learning in healthcare is not without challenges. Data privacy and security are paramount, given the sensitive nature of medical data. Ensuring the ethical use of patient data and compliance with regulations like HIPAA is crucial.

Additionally, the "black box" nature of deep learning models poses a challenge in clinical settings, where understanding the rationale behind a diagnosis or treatment recommendation is essential. Efforts to increase the interpretability of these models are ongoing and crucial for their wider acceptance in medical practice.

Retail: Transforming Customer Experiences and Supply Chain Efficiency

Deep learning is rapidly transforming the retail landscape, driving innovations in customer experience, inventory management, and personalized marketing. This technology enables retailers to harness vast amounts of data, uncovering insights that lead to more efficient operations and a more customized shopping experience. The following case studies illustrate the profound impact of deep learning in retail.

The application of deep learning in retail is extensive, offering solutions that range from improving customer engagement to optimizing supply chains. Deep learning models can analyze customer data, including past purchases, browsing habits, and social media interactions, to predict future buying behaviors, tailor recommendations, and ensure product availability aligns with consumer demand.

Case Study 1: Personalized Recommendations on an E-commerce Platform

A leading e-commerce giant transformed its recommendation system by integrating deep learning, significantly enhancing customer engagement and boosting sales.

> **Challenge**: The platform struggled with the accuracy of its previous recommendation system, often suggesting products that failed to resonate with individual customers' tastes and preferences. This led to lost sales opportunities and diminished user engagement.

> **Solution**: The company developed a deep learning-based recommendation engine that analyzes extensive datasets, including past purchase history, items viewed, customer reviews, and even time spent on product pages. This engine utilized a combination of CNNs for image analysis and RNNs

to understand sequential patterns in browsing and purchasing behaviors.

Outcome: The new recommendation system drastically improved the relevance of product suggestions, leading to a significant increase in customer engagement and sales. Personalized marketing messages became more effective, increasing conversion rates and customer satisfaction. The success of this system set a new standard in e-commerce, prompting others in the industry to adopt similar deep learning-based approaches.

Case Study 2: Optimizing Inventory Management for a Retail Chain

A multinational retail chain utilized deep learning to revolutionize its inventory management, addressing overstock and stockout issues that plagued its operations.

Challenge: The retailer faced recurring problems with inventory levels across its stores, leading to frequent stockouts of popular items and overstocks of less popular products, resulting in lost sales and increased holding costs.

Solution: The company implemented a deep learning model that analyzed sales data, seasonal trends, promotional activities, and even local events likely to affect demand. The model provided highly accurate predictions of product demand at individual store levels, allowing for more precise inventory planning and distribution.

Outcome: The deep learning-powered inventory system significantly reduced stockouts and overstocks, improving customer satisfaction by ensuring product availability and reducing inventory costs. The efficiency gained from this system contributed to the retailer's ability to offer competitive pricing and maintain profitability.

Case Study 3: Enhancing In-Store Customer Experience with Deep Learning

A fashion retailer sought to enhance the in-store shopping experience by integrating deep learning into its customer service operations.

Challenge: In an increasingly digital shopping environment, the retailer aimed to attract more customers to its physical stores by offering a uniquely personalized shopping experience.

Solution: The retailer deployed a deep learning-based system that analyzed real-time in-store video feeds to understand customer behaviors and preferences. The system identified when customers appeared to need assistance or were interested in particular products, alerting staff to provide timely and relevant support. Additionally, it analyzed foot traffic patterns to optimize store layouts and product placements.

Outcome: Implementing this system led to a marked improvement in customer service, with store staff able to provide more personalized and efficient assistance. Optimizing store layouts based on deep learning analysis also increased sales per square foot, demonstrating the tangible benefits of enhancing the in-store experience through technology.

Impact and Implications

These case studies underscore deep learning's transformative potential in retail, from personalizing the online shopping experience to optimizing inventory management and enhancing the in-store experience. By leveraging deep learning's predictive power, retailers can improve operational efficiencies and deepen customer engagement, increasing loyalty and sales.

Challenges and Considerations

Despite the benefits, integrating deep learning into retail operations presents challenges, including ensuring customer data privacy and navigating the complexities of implementing AI technologies in legacy systems. Retailers must also contend with the need for continuous model training and updating to keep pace with changing consumer behaviors and market trends.

Manufacturing: Predictive Maintenance and Quality Control

Integrating deep learning in manufacturing is revolutionizing the industry, enhancing operational efficiency, and ensuring product quality through predictive maintenance and advanced quality control. This transformative approach leverages the power of deep learning models, particularly Convolutional Neural Networks (CNNs), to analyze real-time data from manufacturing equipment, predict potential failures, and identify quality defects with unprecedented accuracy.

Adopting deep learning in manufacturing is part of the broader movement toward Industry 4.0, which emphasizes digitalization, data integration, and automation. In this context, deep learning is a critical tool for predictive maintenance and quality control, two areas where the ability to analyze vast amounts of data can significantly improve efficiency and product quality.

Predictive maintenance represents a proactive approach to equipment maintenance, identifying and addressing potential issues before they lead to failures. Deep learning models, trained on historical equipment data, sensor readings, and operational parameters, can detect subtle patterns and anomalies that signal impending failures. This predictive capability allows manufacturers to schedule maintenance more effectively, minimizing unplanned downtime and extending the lifespan of their equipment.

Deep learning models, particularly CNNs, are employed in quality control to inspect products for defects. These models are trained on images of defective and non-defective products, learning to identify discrepancies that may indicate quality issues. This automated quality control approach increases defects' detection rate and reduces reliance on manual inspections, which can be time-consuming and less consistent.

Case Study 1: Automobile Manufacturer Implements CNN-based Inspection System

An international automobile manufacturer faced challenges maintaining consistent quality across its assembly line products. The reliance on manual inspections led to variability in defect detection rates and, consequently, inconsistencies in product quality.

Challenge: An international automobile manufacturer grappled with ensuring consistent quality due to variability in manual defect detection, leading to inconsistencies in product quality across its assembly line.

Solution: The company implemented a CNN-based inspection system to automate the quality control process. The system was trained on thousands of images capturing various assembly line products, both defective and non-defective, allowing it to learn the characteristics of a quality product.

Outcome: The CNN-based system significantly outperformed human inspectors in defect detection, identifying issues with higher precision and consistency. This led to a notable reduction in manufacturing errors, ensuring product quality and enhancing brand reputation. Additionally, the system's ability to operate continuously resulted in faster inspection times, increasing production efficiency.

Case Study 2: Predictive Maintenance in Semiconductor Manufacturing

A leading semiconductor manufacturer sought to improve the uptime of its complex manufacturing equipment, which was prone to unexpected failures, causing costly production delays.

Challenge: A semiconductor manufacturer faced frequent, unpredictable equipment failures, leading to costly delays and impacting manufacturing productivity and efficiency.
Solution: The company deployed deep learning models to analyze real-time data from equipment sensors, including vibration, temperature, and pressure readings. These models were trained to identify patterns indicative of equipment wear or impending failures, allowing for timely maintenance interventions.
Outcome: The predictive maintenance system dramatically reduced equipment downtime by allowing maintenance to be scheduled during planned production pauses. This proactive approach saved costs associated with unplanned maintenance and production losses and improved

overall equipment efficiency (OEE), a critical metric in manufacturing productivity.

Case Study 3: Enhancing Packaging Quality in the Food Industry

A food manufacturing company faced challenges in ensuring the integrity of its packaging, a crucial aspect of product quality and safety. Defects in packaging could lead to product contamination and significant financial and reputational damage.

Challenge: A food manufacturing company struggled to maintain packaging integrity, risking product contamination, financial loss, and damage to its reputation due to packaging defects.

Solution: The company implemented a deep learning system equipped with CNNs to inspect packaging on the production line. The system was trained on a diverse dataset of packaging images, enabling it to detect a wide range of potential defects, from seal irregularities to labeling errors.

Outcome: The deep learning-based inspection system significantly improved the detection rate of

> packaging defects, virtually eliminating instances of compromised product integrity. This enhancement in quality control protected the company from potential recalls and liability issues and bolstered consumer trust in the brand.

Impact and Implications

These case studies exemplify deep learning's profound impact on manufacturing and demonstrate its potential to enhance predictive maintenance and quality control. By leveraging deep learning's predictive power, manufacturers can anticipate and mitigate equipment failures, reducing downtime and maintenance costs. Similarly, applying deep learning in quality control ensures higher product quality and consistency, which is essential for maintaining competitiveness in today's market.

Challenges and Considerations

While deep learning offers vast potential, its application in business is not without challenges. Data privacy is a significant concern, especially in finance and healthcare. Ensuring the security of sensitive information and compliance with regulations such as GDPR is paramount. Additionally, the successful implementation of deep learning projects requires substantial computational resources and specialized expertise, necessitating strategic planning and investment.

Conclusion

Deep learning is redefining what's possible in the business world, offering solutions to longstanding challenges and opening new avenues for innovation. As we've seen through various case studies, its applications span multiple industries, driving efficiency, enhancing customer experiences, and enabling personalized services. For managers and business leaders, understanding and leveraging deep learning is no longer optional but a strategic imperative to stay competitive in the digital era. As we continue to explore its potential, the key to success lies in navigating the challenges thoughtfully, ensuring ethical considerations, and fostering a culture of innovation and continuous learning.

7. Navigating the Ethical and Social Implications

In the burgeoning era of deep learning, managers are increasingly called upon to confront and navigate a labyrinth of ethical and social implications. This chapter delves into the core ethical considerations surrounding deep learning, encompassing data privacy, algorithmic bias, and the profound impact of artificial intelligence on employment. It aims to arm managers with the requisite knowledge to steer these challenges with responsibility and ethical foresight in their deep learning initiatives.

Data Privacy: A Paramount Concern

In the contemporary realm of deep learning, the colossal volumes of data that fuel these advanced algorithms underscore a critical challenge: safeguarding data privacy. Protecting sensitive and personal information is not merely a legal obligation but a cornerstone of ethical AI development.

The Imperative of Data Privacy

The proliferation of deep learning applications across various sectors, from healthcare to finance, has escalated concerns regarding data privacy. Personal data, when mishandled or breached, can lead to significant consequences, affecting individuals' privacy rights and organizations' reputations and financial standing. Managers at the helm of deep learning projects are responsible for implementing stringent measures to ensure data privacy.

Strategies for Upholding Data Privacy

- **Adherence to Legal Standards**: Compliance with international data protection regulations, such as the General Data Protection Regulation (GDPR) in the European Union, is paramount. These regulations provide a legal framework for data handling and protect individuals' rights.
- **Data Encryption**: Implementing state-of-the-art encryption methods for data at rest and in transit shields sensitive information from unauthorized access, providing a robust layer of security.

- **Privacy-First Culture**: Cultivating an organizational culture that prioritizes privacy involves regular training, transparent policies, and a proactive stance on privacy issues, ensuring all team members are aligned in their approach to data handling.

Case Study 1: Healthcare Data Privacy

Challenge: A healthcare startup leveraging deep learning for patient diagnosis faced the dual challenge of utilizing detailed patient data for model training while ensuring uncompromised privacy.
Solution: The startup adopted a privacy-preserving approach, employing techniques like differential privacy, which adds 'noise' to the data, obfuscating individual details without diluting the dataset's overall utility for model training. Additionally, the company implemented robust data encryption and adhered strictly to HIPAA regulations, ensuring patient data was securely managed.
Outcome: The startup successfully developed a deep learning model that enhanced diagnostic accuracy without compromising patient privacy,

setting a precedent for privacy-conscious AI development in healthcare.

Case Study 2: Retail Personalization and Privacy

Challenge: A retail giant sought to personalize customer experiences through deep learning algorithms but grappled with the ethical implications of using personal shopping data, risking customer trust.

Solution: The retailer instituted a transparent opt-in policy for data collection, clearly communicating the benefits and privacy measures to customers. They employed anonymization techniques, ensuring individual customer data could not be traced back to specific individuals. Additionally, the company adhered to GDPR guidelines, granting customers control over their data.

Outcome: The retailer successfully personalized marketing efforts, enhancing customer engagement and sales while maintaining high data privacy standards, thereby strengthening customer trust.

Case Study 3: Financial Services and Secure Data Handling

Challenge: A fintech company using deep learning for fraud detection must process vast amounts of transactional data, which raises significant data privacy concerns.
Solution: The fintech firm implemented a comprehensive encryption strategy, securing data at every point from collection to analysis. They also adopted a principle of data minimization, only collecting data essential for fraud detection and ensuring all data handling practices were in strict compliance with financial regulations and GDPR.
Outcome: The company enhanced its fraud detection capabilities without infringing on customer privacy, bolstering its reputation as a trustworthy financial service provider.

Ethical Considerations and Best Practices

These case studies underscore the necessity of a multi-pronged approach to data privacy in deep learning projects. Ethical considerations should guide the deployment of deep learning technologies, ensuring they serve the greater good while respecting individual privacy rights. Best practices include the following.

- **Regular Privacy Audits**: Conducting periodic audits to assess and improve data handling practices.
- **Stakeholder Engagement**: Involving all stakeholders in discussions about data privacy, ensuring transparency and accountability.
- **Continuous Learning**: Staying abreast of emerging privacy-enhancing technologies and incorporating them into deep learning projects.

Algorithmic Bias: Ensuring Fairness

Algorithmic bias represents one of the most pressing ethical concerns in deep learning. It refers to systematic and unfair discrimination embedded within the outcomes of AI models, often mirroring the biases inherent in their training data. This challenge raises ethical red flags and poses significant risks to businesses regarding credibility, legal compliance, and social responsibility. This comprehensive examination of algorithmic bias will unravel its origins, consequences, and the methodologies to counteract it, as elucidated through three insightful case studies.

Understanding Algorithmic Bias

Deep learning models are fundamentally shaped by the data they are trained on. When this data contains biases - from historical inequalities, societal stereotypes, or skewed sampling - the models can inadvertently learn and perpetuate these biases. This can lead to discriminatory outcomes in various applications, from hiring tools that favor certain demographics to credit scoring systems that unjustly disadvantage specific groups.

Detecting algorithmic bias involves rigorous testing of the model across diverse datasets to identify discriminatory patterns. Mitigation strategies include diversifying training data, employing fairness-aware algorithms, and incorporating ethical oversight throughout the model development lifecycle.

Case Study 1: Fair Hiring in the Tech Industry

Challenge: A tech conglomerate noticed a significant gender disparity in engineering roles. An internal audit revealed that the AI-driven hiring tool was biased, favoring male candidates due to the historical male dominance in the dataset used for training the model.

Solution: The company undertook a comprehensive review of its hiring algorithms, implementing a fairness-aware model that accounted for gender balance. It incorporated a more diverse dataset, including successful candidates from underrepresented genders, and applied debiasing techniques to ensure the model's neutrality.

Outcome: The retrained model significantly reduced gender bias, leading to a more diverse pool of candidates being shortlisted and hired. This enhanced the company's diversity and inclusivity and improved team innovation and performance.

Case Study 2: Equitable Loan Approvals in Banking

Challenge: A multinational bank faced public scrutiny when reports emerged suggesting that its loan approval algorithm discriminated against applicants from specific ethnic backgrounds, a bias inherited from historical loan data.

Solution: The bank collaborated with AI ethics experts to overhaul its loan approval system. This involved cleansing the training data of discriminatory biases, implementing a fairness-oriented algorithmic framework, and introducing continuous monitoring for biased outcomes.

Outcome: The revamped system led to fairer loan approval rates across different demographic groups, restoring customer trust and ensuring compliance with anti-discrimination laws. The bank also established an AI ethics board to oversee all AI deployments, embedding fairness at the core of its operations.

Case Study 3: Bias-Free Advertising in E-commerce

Challenge: An e-commerce giant discovered that its targeted advertising algorithm was unintentionally biased. It disproportionately showed high-paying job ads to male users and domestic product ads to female users, reinforcing harmful stereotypes.

Solution: The e-commerce platform adopted an 'equal opportunity' approach to its advertising algorithms. It involved retraining the models with balanced datasets and applying fairness constraints to ensure that ads were displayed equally across genders.

Outcome: The new approach led to a more equitable distribution of ads, promoting gender neutrality in job and product advertisements. This countered the perpetuation of stereotypes and opened new market segments, enhancing the platform's reach and diversity.

Impact and Best Practices

These case studies underscore the critical need for fairness in AI systems and the tangible steps businesses can take to achieve it. Addressing algorithmic bias involves technical adjustments and fostering an organizational culture prioritizing ethical AI use.

Best practices in mitigating algorithmic bias include the following.

- **Diverse Data Collection**: Ensuring the training data reflects the diversity of the natural world and the application's intended audience.
- **Ethical AI Governance**: Establishing committees or boards to oversee AI projects, ensuring ethical considerations are integrated from inception to deployment.
- **Transparency and Accountability**: Being open about the functioning of AI models, the data they're trained on, and the measures taken to ensure fairness.
- **Continuous Monitoring**: Regularly reviewing AI systems post-deployment to detect and correct emergent biases.

The Impact on Employment: Navigating the Transition

The advent of deep learning and its integration into various sectors has ignited a profound transformation in the employment landscape. While deep learning's automation capabilities promise enhanced efficiency and productivity, they also pose significant challenges to traditional workforce roles, stirring concerns about job displacement and the future of work. This intricate scenario demands a careful navigation strategy, emphasizing reskilling, human-AI collaboration, and supportive policies to facilitate a smooth transition for the workforce.

The Dual-edged Sword of Deep Learning Automation

Deep learning's capacity to automate complex tasks that were once the sole purview of humans marks a significant leap in technological advancement. This automation potential, however, is a double-edged sword. On one hand, it allows businesses to streamline operations, reduce errors, and enhance productivity. On the other hand, it raises existential questions for specific job roles, particularly those involving repetitive or pattern-based tasks that deep learning algorithms can efficiently execute.

The transition induced by deep learning automation necessitates a strategic approach to workforce management. It involves addressing the immediate impacts of automation, envisioning the future work landscape, and preparing the workforce for this new reality. Key strategies include:

- **Reskilling and Upskilling Initiatives**: Investing in employees' continuous learning and development to equip them with relevant skills in an AI-driven workplace.
- **Fostering Human-AI Collaboration**: Redefining job roles to emphasize the collaborative potential between humans and AI, leveraging each's unique strengths.
- **Advocating for Supportive Policies**: Working with policymakers to develop frameworks that support workforce adaptation, such as safety nets for displaced workers and incentives for businesses to invest in employee development.

Case Study 1: Reskilling in the Manufacturing Sector

Challenge: A manufacturing company faced potential workforce displacement due to implementing deep learning-powered automation in its production lines.

Solution: Recognizing the imperative to retain and revalue its human capital, the company launched a comprehensive reskilling program. Employees previously engaged in manual assembly tasks were offered training in AI oversight, maintenance, and data analysis - skills crucial for managing and optimizing automated production systems.

Outcome: The reskilling initiative mitigated job displacement and enriched the workforce's skill set, enhancing the company's overall operational efficiency. Employees transitioned to more fulfilling roles, overseeing the automated systems and contributing to continuous improvement processes.

Case Study 2: Human-AI Collaboration in Healthcare

Challenge: A hospital introduced deep learning algorithms to assist in diagnosing complex diseases, leading to concerns among medical staff about the devaluation of their expertise.

Solution: The hospital emphasized the concept of human-AI collaboration, positioning the deep learning system as a tool to augment, not replace, the medical professionals' expertise. Training sessions demonstrated how AI can enhance diagnostic accuracy and allow healthcare professionals to focus on patient care and complex case management.

Outcome: The collaborative approach significantly improved diagnostic accuracy and patient outcomes. Healthcare professionals reported higher job satisfaction, valuing the AI system as a reliable assistant that enhances their decision-making process.

Case Study 3: Policy Advocacy in the Service Industry

Challenge: A service industry conglomerate recognized the impending impact of AI-driven customer service solutions on its extensive customer support workforce.
Solution: The company took a proactive stance, engaging with industry groups and policymakers to advocate for workforce adaptation policies. This included tax incentives for companies investing in employee reskilling, funding for vocational training programs in AI-related fields, and safety nets for displaced workers.
Outcome: The advocacy efforts led to the implementation of supportive policies that eased the workforce transition, enabling the company and others in the industry to invest in reskilling programs. The workforce was gradually reoriented towards roles that require human empathy and strategic thinking, complementing AI-driven customer service solutions.

Ethical Frameworks and Guidelines

Navigating the ethical implications of deep learning's rapidly evolving landscape is paramount for managers and leaders. Ethical frameworks and guidelines provide a structured approach to moral decision-making and ensure deep learning applications are developed and deployed responsibly. This comprehensive exploration delves into the essence of these ethical tenets, underscored by real-world case studies that illustrate their application in various sectors.

Ethical Tenets in Deep Learning

The ethical deployment of deep learning technology hinges on several core principles.

- **Transparency**: Ensuring that the workings of deep learning models are understandable to stakeholders, including developers, users, and those impacted by their application.
- **Accountability**: Establishing clear lines of responsibility for the outcomes of deep learning systems, ensuring that those

deploying these technologies can be held accountable for their impacts.
- **Stakeholder Engagement**: Involving all parties affected by deep learning applications in the decision-making process, ensuring that diverse perspectives are considered and ethical dilemmas are addressed collaboratively.

Adhering to these principles requires a concerted effort from all involved in the deep learning ecosystem, from data scientists and engineers to policymakers and end-users.

Ethical Frameworks and Guidelines: A Scaffold for Decision-Making

Developing and adhering to ethical frameworks and guidelines in deep learning is not a one-size-fits-all process. It requires a tailored approach that considers the specific applications, stakeholders, and potential impacts of deep learning technologies. Essential components of a practical ethical framework include the following.

- **Principle-Based Approach**: Defining ethical principles that guide developing and deploying deep learning applications, ensuring they align with broader societal values and norms.
- **Stakeholder Analysis**: Identify all parties affected by deep learning applications and consider their perspectives and concerns in decision-making.
- **Ethical Review Processes**: Establishing processes for ethical review and approval of deep learning projects, including assessing potential risks and benefits and strategies for mitigating ethical concerns.
- **Continuous Monitoring and Evaluation**: Implement mechanisms for monitoring deep learning applications on an ongoing basis, ensuring they operate within ethical boundaries and adapt to new insights and challenges.

Conclusion

As deep learning continues to redefine business landscapes, the ethical and social implications it brings to the fore are profound. Managers must navigate these waters with diligence and integrity at the confluence of technology and ethics. This chapter equips them with the insights and tools necessary to embrace deep learning as a technological advancement and a societal responsibility, ensuring its benefits are harnessed ethically and equitably for all.

8. Managing Risks in Deep Learning Projects

Deep learning projects, with their vast potential to revolutionize business operations and decision-making, also introduce a range of risks that managers must adeptly navigate. This chapter delves into the multifaceted dangers of deep learning initiatives, from technical hurdles and security vulnerabilities to legal and ethical considerations. It offers a comprehensive guide for managers on assessing these risks and implementing effective mitigation strategies, ensuring the integrity and success of deep learning projects within their organizations.

Understanding the Risks

Deep learning projects are complex endeavors that involve substantial data processing, sophisticated algorithms, and significant computational resources. The complexity of these systems can give rise to various risks.

- **Technical Challenges**: Deep learning models can be prone to overfitting, underfitting, and other issues compromising performance and reliability.
- **Data Security and Privacy**: The vast amounts of data required to train deep learning models can include sensitive or personal information, posing significant privacy and security risks.
- **Algorithmic Bias**: Models trained on biased data can produce skewed or unfair outcomes, leading to ethical concerns and potential legal ramifications.
- **Legal and Regulatory Compliance**: Deep learning applications must navigate an evolving landscape of data protection, privacy, and AI ethics regulations.

Risk Assessment and Mitigation Strategies

Effective risk management in deep learning projects involves a systematic approach to identifying, assessing, and mitigating potential risks.

- **Risk Identification**: The first step is to conduct a comprehensive assessment to identify all potential risks associated with the deep learning project. This involves reviewing the project scope, data sources, algorithms, and deployment environments.
- **Risk Analysis**: Once risks are identified, the next step is to analyze their potential impact and likelihood. This analysis helps prioritize risks based on their severity and the probability of occurrence.
- **Risk Mitigation**: Developing and implementing strategies to mitigate identified risks is crucial. This can involve technical solutions, process adjustments, and policy changes.

Case Study 1: Overcoming Technical Challenges in Retail

A retail giant implemented a deep learning system for inventory forecasting. The model initially suffered from overfitting, leading to inaccurate predictions.

Mitigation Strategy: The company addressed the overfitting issue by introducing regularization techniques and expanding the training dataset to include a more diverse range of historical sales data. This improved the model's generalization ability, enhancing forecasting accuracy.

Case Study 2: Ensuring Data Privacy in Healthcare

A healthcare provider used deep learning to analyze patient records for disease prediction. Concerns arose regarding the privacy of sensitive patient data.

Mitigation Strategy: The provider implemented robust data anonymization and encryption techniques to protect patient information. They also ensured compliance with healthcare regulations like HIPAA, enhancing data security and patient trust.

Case Study 3: Addressing Algorithmic Bias in Financial Services

A fintech company developed a deep learning model for credit scoring, which was later found to be biased against certain demographic groups.

Mitigation Strategy: The company conducted a thorough audit of the training data and model algorithms to identify sources of bias. They then retrained the model with a more balanced dataset and implemented fairness constraints to ensure equitable credit-scoring outcomes.

Fostering a Risk-Aware Culture

Managing risks in deep learning projects requires technical and strategic measures and fostering a risk-aware culture within the organization. This involves the following.

- **Continuous Learning**: Encouraging teams to stay updated on the latest deep learning advancements, potential risks, and mitigation techniques.
- **Collaboration**: Promoting cross-functional partnerships between data scientists, engineers, legal experts, and ethicists to address risks comprehensively.
- **Ethical Consideration**: Integrating ethical considerations into every stage of the deep

learning project lifecycle, ensuring that models are developed and deployed responsibly.

Conclusion

Navigating the risks associated with deep learning projects is a critical competency for managers in the digital age. By understanding the potential challenges, implementing robust risk assessment and mitigation strategies, and fostering a culture of collaboration and ethical consideration, managers can steer their deep learning initiatives toward success while safeguarding their organizations against potential pitfalls. This chapter equips managers with the knowledge and tools necessary to confidently manage the complexities and risks of deep learning projects, ensuring their transformative potential is realized ethically and effectively.

9. Building a Deep Learning Team

As the transformative power of deep learning continues to be realized across industries, managers' imperative to assemble skilled teams capable of harnessing this technology has never been more critical. This chapter provides a comprehensive guide to building a deep learning team, covering the essential roles and expertise needed and the significance of cultivating a collaborative environment and a culture of continuous learning.

Understanding the Deep Learning Team Dynamics

Deep learning projects demand a multidisciplinary approach, combining expertise in data science, engineering, domain-specific knowledge, and ethical considerations. A successful deep-learning team is not merely a collection of individuals with technical prowess but a cohesive unit that collaborates effectively, shares knowledge, and continuously adapts to new challenges.

Essential Roles in a Deep Learning Team

The essential roles in a Deep Learning Team are mentioned below.

- **Data Scientists**: Specialists who develop deep learning models. They possess a strong foundation in mathematics, statistics, and machine learning. Their role involves experimenting with different models, tuning algorithms, and optimizing performance.
- **Data Engineers**: Responsible for the data pipeline, data engineers ensure that the team can access clean, structured, and reliable data. They manage databases, data storage solutions, and data preprocessing efforts.
- **Machine Learning Engineers**: They focus on bringing the models developed by data scientists into production. This role involves coding, integrating models with existing systems, and ensuring they run efficiently at scale.
- **Domain Experts**: Individuals with deep knowledge of the specific field where deep learning is applied, such as healthcare, finance, or retail. They provide insights into the nuances

of the domain, helping to guide model development and ensure its relevance.
- **Project Managers**: They oversee the project's progress, ensuring milestones are met, resources are allocated effectively, and communication channels are open between team members.
- **Ethical AI Advisors**: With the increasing awareness of AI's ethical implications, it is crucial to have an expert focused on ensuring that deep learning models are developed and deployed responsibly.

Fostering Collaboration and Continuous Learning

Building a deep learning team extends beyond assembling individuals with the right skill sets; it involves nurturing an environment that encourages collaboration, innovation, and continuous growth.

- **Cross-functional Collaboration**: Encouraging regular interactions and knowledge sharing between team members with different

expertise fosters a more integrated approach to problem-solving and innovation.
- **Continuous Learning Culture**: Deep learning is a rapidly evolving field. It is vital to encourage team members to stay abreast of the latest research, tools, and techniques through workshops, conferences, and online courses.
- **Innovative Mindset**: Encourage experimentation and risk-taking within the team. Not every experiment will succeed, but each attempt is an opportunity to learn and innovate.

Case Study 1: Tech Giant's AI Lab

In the rapidly evolving landscape of artificial intelligence, A, a tech behemoth, recognized the imperative to stay at the forefront of innovation. To this end, the company inaugurated an AI lab dedicated to exploring the frontiers of deep learning technology. This initiative wasn't just about technological advancement; it was a strategic move to cultivate an interdisciplinary nexus that could unlock unprecedented capabilities in AI.

Interdisciplinary Synergy

The AI lab at A was not a conventional setup restricted to computer scientists and data analysts. Instead, it represented a melting pot of expertise, pulling in professionals from linguistics, neuroscience, psychology, and more. This diversity was predicated on the understanding that the future of AI would hinge not just on algorithms and computing power but on insights gleaned from how humans think, communicate, and perceive the world.

Linguistics and Natural Language Processing (NLP)

One of the lab's early focuses was enhancing natural language processing (NLP) capabilities. Linguists in the team brought a deep understanding of syntax, semantics, and phonetics, which proved invaluable in developing models that could comprehend and generate human-like text. For instance, leveraging their expertise, the lab developed an AI model capable of understanding context and nuance in language, far surpassing the capabilities of existing NLP systems. This model was instrumental in improving A's voice assistants, making them more intuitive and responsive to complex user queries.

Neuroscience and Computer Vision

Another groundbreaking project involved applying deep learning to computer vision, drawing heavily on neuroscience. Neuroscientists on the team provided insights into how the human brain processes visual information, which informed the development of more advanced convolutional neural networks (CNNs). These networks were designed to mimic the hierarchical way the human visual cortex operates, significantly improving image recognition and classification.

A notable example of this collaboration was developing an AI system capable of "seeing" and interpreting medical images, such as MRIs and CT scans, with a degree of precision comparable to that of trained radiologists. This system not only enhanced diagnostic processes but also served as a tool for medical research, aiding in identifying subtle patterns associated with various diseases.

Fostering Innovation Through Collaboration

The success of the AI lab was not solely a result of the diverse expertise present but also the collaborative ethos that permeated its operations. Open forums, cross-disciplinary teams, and shared projects encouraged a free exchange of ideas, fostering an environment where innovation flourished.

Continuous Learning and Adaptation

The AI lab also strongly emphasized continuous learning and adaptation. Regular workshops, seminars, and guest lectures from leading academics and industry experts kept the team abreast of the latest developments in AI and related fields. This learning culture ensured that the lab's projects were not only cutting-edge but also relevant to evolving technological landscapes and societal needs.

Impact and Future Directions

The interdisciplinary approach of A's AI lab yielded numerous breakthroughs in deep learning applications, significantly impacting various sectors.

In NLP, the advancements led to more sophisticated conversational AI, enhancing customer service bots and virtual assistants. In computer vision, the innovations propelled advances in autonomous vehicles, security surveillance, and healthcare diagnostics.

Looking forward, the lab is exploring the integration of AI with other emerging technologies like quantum computing and blockchain, aiming to unlock new possibilities in data security, computational efficiency, and beyond.

Conclusion

A's AI lab is a testament to the power of interdisciplinary collaboration in pushing the boundaries of what's possible in deep learning and AI. By bringing together diverse expertise and fostering a culture of innovation and continuous education, the lab has achieved remarkable technological breakthroughs and set a blueprint for how future AI research and development can be approached for maximal impact.

Case Study 2: Healthcare Start-up

At the dynamic intersection of healthcare and technology, a pioneering healthcare start-up, MediTech Innovations (the name is fictitious for reference only), embarked on a mission to transform medical diagnostics through deep learning. Recognizing the limitations of traditional diagnostic tools, which often rely heavily on the subjective interpretation of medical imaging, MediTech Innovations sought to harness the objective analytical power of AI to enhance accuracy and efficiency in disease diagnosis.

Building a Multidisciplinary Team

Central to MediTech Innovations' approach was assembling a multidisciplinary team that bridged the gap between medicine and machine learning. This team is comprised of the following personnel.

- **Radiologists**: With years of experience interpreting medical images, radiologists provided crucial insights into the nuances of diagnosing diseases from imaging data, guiding the development of AI models that focus on clinically relevant features.

- **Data Scientists**: With expertise in handling vast datasets and applying complex algorithms, data scientists worked on preprocessing imaging data, ensuring it was in a format conducive to model training and analysis.
- **Machine Learning Engineers**: Specializing in translating algorithms into working models, machine learning engineers focused on developing and refining deep learning models, optimizing them for accuracy and speed.

Pioneering Diagnostic Solutions

MediTech Innovations embarked on several projects that leveraged the unique strengths of its diverse team, leading to breakthroughs in medical diagnostics.

Enhanced Cancer Detection

One of the first projects undertaken was to improve the detection of cancerous tumors in medical imaging. The team developed a CNN-based model trained on thousands of annotated images of cancerous and non-cancerous tissues. The radiologists' expertise ensured that the model was trained on clinically relevant features, while the data scientists and machine learning engineers fine-tuned the model's performance.

The result was an AI diagnostic tool that could identify tumors with a higher degree of sensitivity and specificity than traditional methods, aiding in the early detection and treatment of cancer.

Cardiovascular Disease Prediction

Another project focused on predicting cardiovascular diseases using deep learning to analyze echocardiograms. The interdisciplinary team developed a model to detect subtle patterns in echocardiogram data indicative of early-stage heart disease, which might be overlooked in standard diagnostic processes.

This tool gave cardiologists a powerful adjunct to their diagnostic toolkit, enabling more timely and accurate diagnoses of cardiovascular conditions.

Automating Radiology Reports

Recognizing the workload challenges radiologists face, MediTech Innovations also developed an AI system capable of generating preliminary radiology reports. By training a deep learning model on a vast corpus of radiology reports annotated by experienced radiologists, the system learned to create reports that highlighted critical findings from medical images.

While not replacing human expertise, this tool significantly streamlined the radiology workflow, allowing radiologists to focus on complex cases and patient care.

Fostering Collaboration and Innovation

The success of MediTech Innovations was not just a product of individual expertise but the result of a collaborative culture that encouraged knowledge sharing and cross-disciplinary innovation. Regular team meetings, joint problem-solving sessions, and a shared digital workspace facilitated the exchange of ideas and the integration of medical insights with AI development.

Impact on Healthcare

The deep-learning diagnostic tools developed by MediTech Innovations have profoundly impacted patient care.

- **Early Disease Detection**: The enhanced accuracy in diagnosing diseases like cancer and cardiovascular conditions has enabled earlier interventions, improving patient outcomes.
- **Increased Diagnostic Efficiency**: Automating aspects of the diagnostic process, such as preliminary report generation, has alleviated the workload on healthcare professionals, allowing for more efficient patient care.
- **Data-Driven Insights**: The aggregation and analysis of diagnostic data by AI tools have provided valuable insights into disease patterns and treatment outcomes, informing clinical research and practice.

Conclusion

MediTech Innovations exemplifies the transformative potential of deep learning in healthcare, demonstrating how an interdisciplinary team can develop AI tools that revolutionize medical diagnostics. By blending medical expertise with AI innovation, the start-up has not only advanced the field of medical imaging analysis. Still, it has also set a new standard for patient care, underscoring the critical role of collaboration in harnessing the power of deep learning for societal benefit.

Case Study 3: Financial Services Firm

In an era where digital financial transactions are ubiquitous, the specter of fraud looms large, posing significant challenges to the integrity and trustworthiness of financial services. Recognizing the critical need for an advanced fraud detection system that could operate in real-time, a prominent financial services firm, herein referred to as "FinSecure," embarked on a strategic initiative to harness the power of deep learning to safeguard customer transactions.

Assembling a Specialized Deep Learning Team

Central to FinSecure's approach was forming a dedicated deep learning team, a diverse group of professionals with complementary skills and a shared commitment to ethical AI development.

- **Data Engineers**: Tasked with constructing and managing a robust data infrastructure, these engineers ensured that the deep learning models had access to high-quality, real-time transaction data, enabling effective fraud detection.
- **Machine Learning Engineers**: These experts focused on developing and refining deep learning models, employing advanced algorithms to analyze transaction patterns and identify potential fraud.
- **Financial Analysts**: With their profound understanding of financial transactions and fraud mechanisms, these analysts provided invaluable insights into the types of fraud the models needed to detect, enhancing the system's accuracy and relevance.
- **Ethical AI Advisors**: Given the high stakes in fraud detection, including the potential for

false positives that could unjustly flag legitimate transactions as fraudulent, ethical AI advisors ensured that the development and deployment of the models adhered to the highest ethical standards.

Innovations in Fraud Detection

The collaborative efforts of FinSecure's deep learning team led to several innovative solutions that significantly enhanced the firm's fraud detection capabilities.

- **Adaptive Fraud Detection Models:** Leveraging deep learning's versatility, the team developed adaptive models capable of learning from new and evolving fraud patterns. This dynamic approach ensured the system remained effective even as fraudsters adapted their tactics.
- **Real-Time Analysis:** The integration of real-time data processing allowed the models to analyze transactions as they occurred, providing immediate alerts for suspicious activity. This capability was crucial in

preventing fraud before it could inflict financial damage.

- **Minimizing False Positives**: Recognizing the inconvenience and potential customer dissatisfaction caused by false positives, the team employed sophisticated algorithms to discern legitimate transactions from fraudulent ones with high precision. This balance minimized disruptions to genuine transactions while maintaining vigilant fraud detection.

Ethical Considerations and Customer Trust

In developing the fraud detection system, FinSecure strongly emphasized ethical AI practices. The team implemented measures to ensure transparency, accountability, and fairness in the system's operation.

- **Transparency**: FinSecure communicated openly with customers about using AI in monitoring transactions, ensuring that customers were aware of and consented to these practices.

- **Accountability**: The firm established clear protocols for addressing issues arising from the fraud detection system, including mechanisms for customers to report and resolve false positives.
- **Fairness**: Ethical AI advisors worked to ensure that the models were free from biases that could lead to discriminatory practices, safeguarding against unfair treatment of any customer group.

Impact on Financial Security and Customer Experience

The deep learning-based fraud detection system developed by FinSecure profoundly impacted the firm and its customers.

- **Enhanced Security**: The system's real-time, adaptive capabilities significantly reduced the incidence of fraud, protecting customers' financial assets and the firm's reputation.
- **Improved Customer Experience**: By minimizing false positives, the system ensured that legitimate transactions were processed

smoothly, enhancing customer satisfaction and trust in FinSecure's services.
- **Operational Efficiency**: Automating fraud detection processes allowed FinSecure to allocate human resources more effectively, focusing on strategic initiatives and customer service.

Conclusion

FinSecure's deep learning initiative exemplifies the transformative potential of AI in financial services, particularly in the critical domain of fraud detection. By assembling a multidisciplinary team committed to ethical AI development, the firm created a system that advanced its fraud detection capabilities and reinforced its dedication to customer security and trust. This case study underscores the importance of strategic team composition, ethical considerations, and continuous innovation in leveraging deep learning to address complex challenges in the financial sector.

Conclusion

Assembling a deep learning team is a strategic endeavor that requires thoughtful consideration of the roles and expertise needed and a commitment to fostering a collaborative and innovative environment. By embracing these principles, managers can build teams that are not only technically proficient but also adaptable and ethically aware, positioning their organizations at the forefront of the deep learning revolution.

10. The Future of Deep Learning

As we stand on the precipice of technological innovation, deep learning remains a beacon of progress, driving advancements that once resided in science fiction. This chapter ventures into the horizon of deep learning, exploring emerging trends and breakthrough technologies and their potential to reshape industries, society, and the fabric of our digital existence.

Advancements in Neural Network Architectures

The evolution of neural network architectures is at the heart of deep learning's future. New architectures like Capsule Networks (CapsNets), which propose more dynamic routing between layers, promise to overcome CNNs' limitations in understanding spatial hierarchies.

Another frontier is the development of Spiking Neural Networks (SNNs), which mimic how biological neurons function, offering potential leaps in efficiency and performance. These advancements suggest a future where deep learning models can process information more akin to human cognition, enabling more nuanced interpretations of complex data.

Transfer Learning and Democratization of AI

Transfer learning, the practice of applying knowledge gained in one domain to another, is poised to democratize deep learning. Pre-trained models, accessible through platforms like TensorFlow Hub, allow businesses and developers to leverage state-of-the-art models without the prohibitive costs of training from scratch. This democratization will enable smaller enterprises and startups to innovate, bringing deep learning applications to various industries and niches.

Integration with Quantum Computing

The nascent field of quantum computing holds promise for solving deep learning's most significant challenges, particularly in computational efficiency. Quantum algorithms have the potential to perform complex calculations at unprecedented speeds, making it feasible to train more extensive, more sophisticated models. This synergy between deep learning and quantum computing could usher in a new era of AI capabilities, from drug discovery to solving intricate optimization problems.

Personalized and Predictive Medicine

In healthcare, deep learning is set to revolutionize personalized and predictive medicine. Models that can analyze genetic information, lifestyle data, and medical histories could provide personalized health insights and treatment plans tailored to the individual's unique biological makeup. This precision medicine approach could significantly improve chronic disease management and preventive care outcomes.

Autonomous Systems and Robotics

The fusion of deep learning with robotics is forging the path for advanced autonomous systems. Beyond autonomous vehicles, which continue to benefit from deep learning in navigation and decision-making, we're seeing the emergence of robots that can learn and adapt to complex environments. The applications are vast and varied, from precision agriculture to autonomous drones for disaster response.

Ethical AI and Governance

As deep learning technologies become more embedded in our lives, the emphasis on ethical AI and robust governance frameworks will intensify. Future developments will likely include more sophisticated methods for ensuring AI systems' transparency, fairness, and accountability. This could involve novel approaches to model interpretability and standards and regulations that guide the ethical deployment of AI technologies.

The Impact on Employment and Education

The implications of deep learning on the workforce and educational systems are profound. As automation and AI capabilities advance, there's a growing need for reskilling and upskilling initiatives to prepare the workforce for a future where human-AI collaboration is commonplace. Similarly, educational curricula will need to evolve, emphasizing critical thinking, creativity, and digital literacy to complement the capabilities of AI systems.

Conclusion

The future of deep learning is a tapestry of promise and challenge, woven with advancements in technology, shifts in societal norms, and the perpetual quest for knowledge. For managers and business leaders, staying abreast of these trends is not just advantageous—it's imperative. Embracing the future of deep learning requires a vision that extends beyond the horizon, anticipating changes, fostering innovation, and navigating the ethical landscape with integrity. As we chart the course of deep learning's future, it's clear that its potential is only limited by our imagination, ethics, and willingness to adapt. This chapter serves as a compass, guiding managers through the uncharted territories of deep learning's promising yet unpredictable future.

11. Preparing Your Organization for Deep Learning

In an era when deep learning is setting new benchmarks for innovation across industries, organizations must adapt to fully leverage its potential. This chapter offers managers pragmatic insights into preparing their organizations for integrating and adopting deep learning technologies. It encompasses strategic planning, infrastructure development, and fostering a culture of innovation, providing a comprehensive roadmap for harnessing the transformative power of deep learning.

Strategic Planning for Deep Learning Integration

The first step in preparing your organization for deep learning is strategic planning. This involves understanding your organization's needs and how deep learning can address them.

- **Assess Organizational Needs**: Identify areas where deep learning can significantly impact, such as improving product offerings, optimizing operations, or enhancing customer experiences.
- **Set Clear Objectives**: Define what you aim to achieve with deep learning. Objectives could range from increasing efficiency and reducing costs to driving innovation and gaining a competitive edge.
- **Develop a Roadmap**: Outline a step-by-step plan for integrating deep learning into your operations, including timelines, milestones, and key performance indicators (KPIs).

Building the Infrastructure for Deep Learning

Deep learning requires a robust technological infrastructure to support the intensive computational processes.

- **Hardware Considerations**: Assess the need for specialized hardware, such as GPUs or

TPUs, which are critical for efficiently training deep learning models.
- **Data Infrastructure**: Ensure you have a solid data infrastructure in place. This includes reliable data storage solutions and effective data management practices to handle the large volumes of data deep learning models require.
- **Cloud Computing and Scalability**: Consider cloud computing solutions that offer scalability and flexibility. Cloud platforms can provide access to state-of-the-art hardware and software, facilitating the deployment and scaling of deep learning models.

Cultivating a Culture of Innovation

Deep learning must thrive within a culture that embraces innovation, continuous learning, and collaboration.

- **Foster Continuous Learning**: Encourage employees to stay abreast of the latest advancements in deep learning and related fields. This can be facilitated through training

programs, workshops, and participation in relevant conferences.
- **Promote Cross-Disciplinary Collaboration:** Deep learning projects often require collaboration across different departments and specialties. Promote a culture where data scientists, domain experts, and business leaders work together towards common goals.
- **Encourage Experimentation:** Create an environment where experimentation is encouraged, and failure is seen as an opportunity to learn. This approach fosters innovation and can lead to groundbreaking applications of deep learning.

Examples of Organizational Preparation for Deep Learning

I am providing some real cases of organizations adopting Deep Learning technology. The company names have been anonymized.

Example 1: Retail Chain's Personalization Project

A global retail chain wanted to use deep learning to personalize shopping experiences. The company conducted an organizational audit to identify gaps in its data infrastructure and technical capabilities. It then invested in training its IT team in data engineering practices suited for deep learning. It set up a dedicated AI lab where data scientists and marketing experts collaborated to develop personalization algorithms. The project significantly increased customer engagement and sales.

Example 2: Healthcare Provider's Diagnostic Tool

A healthcare provider aimed to implement deep learning to enhance diagnostic tools. The organization focused on creating an extensive database of anonymized patient images and diagnostics. It also established partnerships with tech companies to access advanced computational resources. An interdisciplinary team, including medical professionals, data scientists, and ethicists, was formed to guide the project, ensuring that the tools developed were ethically sound and clinically valuable.

Example 3: Manufacturing Firm's Quality Control Initiative

A manufacturing firm planned to use deep learning for quality control in its production line. The company upgraded its data storage and processing capabilities to recognize the need for a robust infrastructure. It also launched a series of workshops to familiarize its engineering team with deep learning concepts. A pilot project was initiated, demonstrating significant improvements in defect detection rates, paving the way for a company-wide rollout.

Conclusion

Preparing your organization for deep learning requires thoughtful planning, infrastructure investment, and a commitment to fostering an innovative culture. By aligning deep learning initiatives with organizational goals, investing in the necessary technological foundations, and creating an environment that encourages learning and collaboration, managers can unlock the full potential of deep learning to drive their organization forward.

12. Embracing the Deep Learning Era

As we conclude our journey through the realms of deep learning, it is evident that this technology is not just a fleeting trend but a profound revolution reshaping the landscape of industries and businesses across the globe. Deep learning stands at the confluence of data, computing power, and innovative algorithms, offering unprecedented opportunities for organizations willing to embrace its potential.

Key Takeaways

Fundamental Understanding: At its core, deep learning is about learning from data. The foundational concepts of neurons, networks, weights, and biases form the building blocks of systems that can learn, adapt, and make decisions with increasing autonomy.

Technological Advancements: The deep learning revolution is propelled by breakthroughs in algorithms and computational hardware, making tasks that were

once deemed impossible for machines - like understanding human speech, recognizing images, and predicting complex patterns - now within reach.

Practical Applications: From finance and healthcare to retail and manufacturing, deep learning is driving efficiencies, enhancing decision-making, and creating new value propositions. Its applications are as diverse as the industries it permeates, each leveraging the technology to solve unique challenges and innovate.

Ethical Considerations: Deep learning adoption comes with significant ethical responsibilities. Issues of data privacy, algorithmic bias, and the impact on employment demand thoughtful consideration and action from managers and leaders to ensure technology is used responsibly.

Risk Management: Deep learning projects have inherent risks like any technological endeavor. Technical challenges, security vulnerabilities, and legal implications require robust risk assessment and mitigation strategies to safeguard project success and integrity.

The Importance of Teams: Building a skilled deep-learning team is crucial. A blend of data scientists, engineers, domain experts, and ethical advisors can drive projects from conception to successful implementation, fostering a collaborative and innovative environment.

Future Prospects: The future of deep learning is vibrant and filled with potential. Emerging trends, such as advancements in neural network architectures and the integration with technologies like quantum computing, hint at an even more transformative impact on business and society.

Embracing Deep Learning in Your Organization

For managers and leaders, the message is clear: deep learning represents a strategic asset that can provide a competitive edge in today's digital age. Embracing deep learning requires more than just technical adoption; it calls for a strategic vision that aligns with your organization's goals, a commitment to ethical practices, and a culture that champions innovation and continuous learning.

Steps Forward

Stay Informed: The field of deep learning is evolving rapidly. Staying informed about the latest research, tools, and best practices is essential for effectively leveraging the technology.

Foster Talent: Invest in building and nurturing a diverse team with the skills and knowledge to drive your deep learning initiatives. Encourage continuous learning and provide opportunities for team members to explore and innovate.

Ethical Leadership: As a manager, lead by example in ethical AI use. Develop and implement guidelines and practices that ensure your deep learning applications are fair, transparent, and respectful of privacy.

Strategic Integration: Look for opportunities to integrate deep learning into your business processes where it can add the most value. This might involve improving customer experiences, optimizing operations, or creating new products and services.

Conclusion

The deep learning era is upon us, offering a canvas for innovation and transformation. For managers and business leaders, the opportunity to harness this technology to drive growth, enhance decision-making, and create new value is immense. By embracing deep learning with a strategic, ethical, and innovative approach, organizations can not only navigate the challenges of the digital age but also shape the future of their industries. As we look ahead, the potential of deep learning is limited only by our imagination, ethics, and willingness to embrace change. Let this book serve as a guide and an inspiration for you to lead your organization confidently into the deep learning era, unlocking new possibilities and achieving unprecedented success.

About the Author

Partha Majumdar is just a programmer.

Partha has a passion for sharing knowledge. He documents his experiences in technical and management aspects in his blog, http://www.parthamajumdar.org. He also regularly publishes videos on his YouTube channel, https://www.youtube.com/channel/UCbzrZ_aeyiYVo1WJKhlP5sQ.

Partha has continued to learn new domains and technology throughout his career. After graduating in Mathematics, Partha completed a master's in Telecommunications, a master's in Computer Security, and a master's in Information Technology. He has also completed two Executive MBAs in Information Systems and Business Analytics. He completed a PG Certificate program in AI/ML/DL from Manipal Academy of Higher Education (Dubai), an advanced certificate in Cyber Security from IIT (Kanpur), and a PG-level advanced certificate in Computational Data Sciences from IISc (Bengaluru). He is pursuing a Doctorate in Business Administration from the Swiss School of Business and Management (Geneva).

Books by the Author

Learn Emotion Analysis with R

This book is a comprehensive guide to Emotion Analysis using Lexicons, offering a step-by-step code walkthrough for developing Sentiment and Emotion Analysis systems with data from WhatsApp and Twitter. It introduces R and Shiny programming, essential for building emotion analysis systems. The discussion then extends to the fundamentals of Sentiment and Emotion Analysis, leading to the creation of Shiny applications tailored for this purpose. The book concludes by developing a specialized tool for analyzing emotions from Twitter and WhatsApp data. Additionally, it hints at advancing into Machine Learning for Emotion Analysis, contingent on the availability of labeled data, positioning this as a subsequent step for readers.

Link in Amazon Store: https://www.amazon.com/dp/B096K2SVF2

Mastering Classification Algorithms for Machine Learning

This book delves into the core of machine learning through the lens of classification algorithms, which play a pivotal role in categorizing input based on its features. These algorithms are the backbone of various applications, from spam detection to fraud prevention. Starting with a foundational overview of problem-solving in machine learning, the book transitions to a focused examination of classification challenges. It provides an in-depth exploration of the Naïve Bayes algorithm, Logistic Regression, including the crucial sigmoid function, and Decision Trees, highlighting key concepts like the Gini Factor and Entropy. Furthermore, it elaborates on the Random Forest algorithm and concludes with an insightful discussion on Boosting techniques, offering a comprehensive guide to mastering classification algorithms in machine learning.

Link in Amazon Store: https://www.amazon.com/dp/935551851X

Machine Learning for Managers

"Machine Learning for Managers" is a comprehensive guide tailored for leaders aiming to leverage machine learning (ML) within their organizations. It simplifies ML concepts, emphasizing strategic applications over technical complexity. The book covers integrating ML into business practices, ethical data use, and real-world industry applications, showcasing ML's role in enhancing operations and innovation. It also provides insights on team building in the ML era, promoting cross-disciplinary collaboration for effective ML adoption. This book is a strategic roadmap for managers to harness ML, driving informed decision-making and positioning their organizations for future success in an AI-driven landscape.

Link in Amazon Store: https://www.amazon.in/dp/B0CZ5XTQ1L

Generative AI for Managers

"Generative AI for Managers" is a cutting-edge guide that demystifies Generative AI for business leaders eager to harness this technology for growth and innovation. It delves into how Generative AI can revolutionize aspects of business, from enhancing customer experiences to optimizing operations and driving strategic decision-making. The book provides a wealth of practical applications, showcases how mundane tasks can be automated for efficiency, and presents strategies for fostering a culture of innovation through AI. Additionally, it offers guidance on the ethical implementation of AI technologies, ensuring they complement and augment human capabilities within the organizational framework, thereby paving the way for a future rich in opportunities and advancements.

Link in Amazon Store: https://www.amazon.in/dp/B0CXYBFJHD

ChatGPT AI for Managers

"ChatGPT for Managers" is a vital resource for leaders navigating the AI revolution, focusing on integrating Generative AI, like ChatGPT, in enhancing managerial functions and team dynamics. It provides practical insights into leveraging ChatGPT to streamline tasks, bolster decision-making, and encourage innovative thinking within teams. This guide transcends theoretical knowledge, offering actionable strategies for managers to complement their skills with AI, thereby elevating their leadership effectiveness. Through real-world applications and expert advice, readers will learn to harmonize traditional management with AI advancements, ensuring they remain at the forefront of the evolving business environment.

Link in Amazon Store: https://www.amazon.in/dp/B0CY8L4CQ9

Recommendation Systems for Managers

"Recommendation Systems for Managers" demystifies the complexities of data-driven recommendation systems in an easy-to-understand format tailored for managers. This insightful guide traverses Time Series and Market Basket Analysis, AI, ML, and emerging technologies, offering a practical roadmap for implementing these systems. It's an indispensable resource for managers aiming to harness recommendation systems for strategic business decisions in the digital age.

Link in Amazon Store: https://www.amazon.in/dp/B0CXNNSJRC

Linear Programming for Project Management Professionals

This guide equips project management professionals with strategies to address project crashing through linear programming, ensuring timely completion and cost efficiency. It starts with foundational project management concepts and progresses to monitoring techniques and linear programming problem (LPP) formulation. The book delves into solving LPPs, highlighting the use of tools like Microsoft Excel's Solver. It offers insights into applying these methods to real-world project crashing scenarios, emphasizing time and cost optimization. Additionally, it explores the integration of earned value management in project crashing, providing a comprehensive toolkit for project management teams to navigate complex project challenges.

Link in Amazon Store: https://www.amazon.com/dp/B09PD1GFMY

Mutual Fund Investing

"Mutual Fund Investing" is a definitive guide designed specifically for middle-class investors in India and beyond, simplifying the intricate world of mutual funds. It thoroughly explains mutual funds, including their types and the critical differences between open-ended and closed funds. The book offers strategic insights into systematic investments, tax implications, and the balance of benefits and drawbacks. It guides readers through assessing risk tolerance, interpreting crucial financial metrics, and making well-informed investment choices. Advanced techniques like Piotrowski's F-Score and Mohanram's G-Score equip investors to build diversified portfolios, evaluate fund performance, and refine their investment strategies. Tailored for beginners and seasoned investors, this book is essential for anyone looking to achieve financial growth and security through mutual funds.

Link in Amazon Store: https://www.amazon.com/dp/B0CYNG6B12

Creating an Investment Portfolio

This book delves into the scientific process of making informed investment decisions, highlighting the importance for individuals and corporations. It explores critical theories and applications in portfolio creation, covering various investment vehicles like fixed deposits, mutual funds, and shares, emphasizing the necessary mathematics. Additionally, it introduces simple yet widely used tools for investment calculations. Designed to be accessible to a broad audience, this book is an invaluable guide for beginners and experienced investors aiming to enhance their understanding and effectiveness in investing.

Link in Amazon Store: https://www.amazon.com/dp/B0CK99SPKZ

Gartner Research Analysis

The book provides a clear framework for leveraging insights from the Gartner Hype-Cycle Report, an essential resource for understanding technological trends. It simplifies identifying and evaluating emerging technologies, their developers, and market readiness. A live case study illustrates practical application while emphasizing the need for comprehensive research beyond the report. Essential for those seeking strategic technological guidance, this book demystifies the complex data presented in the Gartner Hype Cycle.

Link in Amazon Store: https://www.amazon.com/dp/B0CK582Y2M

Essay on the Indian Knowledge System – Part 1

The book delves into the Indian Knowledge System (IKS), a comprehensive approach to compiling, conserving, and disseminating India's rich knowledge heritage across various disciplines such as science, mathematics, social sciences, medicine, philosophy, art, and spirituality. It highlights the global perspective of IKS and its relevance in sharing India's intellectual legacy with the world. The study of Indology, or "Bharatatattva," as it's known in Indian scholarship, further explores the historical, cultural, linguistic, and literary facets of the Indian subcontinent. Through a series of concise essays, this book, one of a trilogy on ancient India, offers insights into Bharatatattva, underscoring India's significant contributions to global knowledge.

Link in Amazon Store: https://www.amazon.com/dp/B0CXNN95TR

Weekend in Jordan

To celebrate their 20th wedding anniversary, the authors embarked on a spontaneous trip to Jordan, making travel arrangements just a week prior. The feasibility of this last-minute adventure was greatly aided by Jordan's visa-on-arrival policy for Indians and many other nationalities, making it an accessible destination for a broad audience. Their weekend in Jordan was filled with memorable experiences, like being in a movie, with the country's stunning beauty leaving a lasting impression. Despite its modest size, Jordan's rich offerings, from Petra's historical wonders to the Dead Sea's unique allure and Amman's vibrant city life, were thoroughly explored. This book recounts their remarkable journey, offering insights into the treasures of Jordan.

Link in Amazon Store: https://www.amazon.com/dp/B0CK5N6B3W

Elephant Ride in Chang Wangpo

In 2022, Thailand saw a significant influx of approximately 11.5 million tourists, underlining tourism's vital role in its economy, contributing around 6% to the Thai GDP. Reflecting on their past residency in Bangkok from 1996 to 1999, the authors seized a chance to revisit Thailand in 2018, noticing considerable changes. An efficient metro system has alleviated the once notorious Bangkok traffic, enhancing city navigation. While many cherished aspects remained, improvements in the road network and increased attractions enriched their experience. Coinciding with their 26th wedding anniversary, the business trip also included leisure exploration in

Bangkok and Kanchanaburi, with a memorable visit to Chang Wangpo, blending nostalgia, discovery, and celebration.

Link in Amazon Store: https://www.amazon.com/dp/B0CKGWH97S

Weekend in South Sikkim

This book offers an insightful exploration into the less-traveled South Sikkim, diverging from the usual tourist trails in North Sikkim, like Gangtok and Nathu La Pass. The authors journey through various captivating destinations, including Tsomgo Lake, Baba Ka Mandir, and the picturesque Temi Tea Gardens. They delve into the cultural and spiritual essence of South Sikkim with visits to Namchi's Char Dham and Samdruptse Monastery, providing a comprehensive overview of the region's diverse attractions. Additionally, the narrative extends to Yangang and the Bengal Safari in Siliguri, West Bengal, enriching the travelogue with varied experiences.

Link in Amazon Store: https://www.amazon.com/dp/B0CKL1DNTJ

Trips to Dubai

This travelogue unveils the multifaceted allure of Dubai, a top-tier tourist hub known for landmarks like the Burj Khalifa and Burj Al Arab, alongside thrilling experiences such as helicopter rides and dolphin encounters at the Atlantis. It extends beyond Dubai, shedding light on Abu Dhabi and Sharjah attractions, like the adrenaline-pumping Ferrari World and the enchanting Desert Safari. The author shares personal adventures, offering insights into the intricacies of visiting Dubai and navigating the Gulf region, making this book a valuable resource for anyone looking to explore the rich experiences Dubai and its neighboring emirates offer.

Link in Amazon Store: https://www.amazon.com/dp/B0CKRYQKDN

1-Day Trips from Bengaluru

From 1975 to 2023, Bengaluru evolved from a retirees' haven to India's Silicon Valley, also renowned as Garden City. While Bengaluru has numerous tourist attractions and activity hubs, the city's vicinity offers many exploration destinations. This book focuses on day-trip-worthy spots around Bengaluru, places steeped in historical and mythological significance. It does not cover prominent cities like Mysuru, Chennai, and Hyderabad, as well as scenic locales like Ooty, Goa, and Kerala, as they need more than a day to tour.

Link in Amazon Store: https://www.amazon.com/dp/B0CLK58KTB

A Trip to the Wagah Border

The Wagah Border, straddling India and Pakistan near Amritsar and Lahore, is famed for its ceremonial displays by border forces, symbolizing hope amidst strained relations. This checkpoint, pivotal for prisoner exchanges, represents a unique reconciliation potential. On festive occasions, friendly exchanges between the forces foster harmony. The book visually explores Chandigarh, Shimla, Amritsar, and the Wagah Border, highlighting their rich cultures and historical importance.

Link in Amazon Store: https://www.amazon.com/dp/B0CLYTQ6PV

Weekend Getaways from Bengaluru

This guidebook enhances the tourism experience in India, emphasizing the country's improved accessibility and facilities that cater to all traveler categories. It outlines explicitly short trips from Bengaluru, covering a mix of destinations accessible by road, rail, and air. The book is a resource for planning 2-, 3-, and 4-day excursions to various South Indian locales and select sites in Maharashtra, featuring popular tourist destinations such as Ooty, Kodaikanal, and Mysuru, as well as revered places of worship like Kukke Subramanya and Dharmasthala. It offers practical travel tips, what to anticipate on journeys and insights into each destination's unique offerings.

Link in Amazon Store: https://www.amazon.com/dp/B0CMNRKWQ9

www.ingramcontent.com/pod-product-compliance
Lightning Source LLC
Chambersburg PA
CBHW052148220526
45471CB00004B/1580